ABU

A Game Maker's Life

A Game Maker's Life

A Hall of Fame
Game Inventor *and*
Executive Tells *the*
Inside Story *of*
the Toy Industry

Jeffrey Breslow *with* Cynthia Beebe

Post Hill
PRESS

A POST HILL PRESS BOOK
ISBN: 978-1-63758-437-8
ISBN (eBook): 978-1-63758-438-5

A Game Maker's Life:
A Hall of Fame Game Inventor and Executive Tells the Inside Story of the Toy Industry
© 2022 by Jeffrey Breslow with Cynthia Beebe
All Rights Reserved

Book cover design concept by Julie Winsberg
Book cover photography by Emilio Leon King

Post Hill Press
New York • Nashville
posthillpress.com

Published in the United States of America
1 2 3 4 5 6 7 8 9 10

Dedicated to my
Seven Breslow Boys
My wonderful three sons
Marc, Michael, and Joseph
Who over the years
Have heard many of these stories
And to my amazing four grandsons
Oscar, Jax, Brooks, and Sloan
Who have brought much joy
To their "Poppy"

Table of Contents

Prologue

On July 27, 1976, I was a thirty-three-year-old partner at the most successful toy design company in the world, Marvin Glass & Associates on LaSalle Street in downtown Chicago. Marvin Glass & Associates invented dozens of classic games and toys, including Mouse Trap, Operation, Simon, and Rock 'Em Sock 'Em Robots. I was the youngest partner by a decade, a toy designer dubbed the "Boy Genius" by Marvin Glass himself. Happily married with two beautiful sons, after a rocky start in high school and college, I felt firmly in control of my wonderful life.

Company founder Marvin Glass was a brilliant but secretive businessman, the Steve Jobs of the toy industry. Marvin had died of complications from a stroke two years earlier, but our company still reigned supreme in the ferociously competitive business. The company employed about sixty people, including partners, toy designers, model makers, and engineers. It was a great but demanding place to work, with sixty- to eighty-hour workweeks the norm.

Marvin had designed our office building like a medieval fortress, with slits for windows, locked doors, restricted access, and a giant walk-in vault for prototypes. Security cameras were everywhere. In his desire to protect his firm's people and ideas, Marvin even had a panic button installed under the receptionist's desk routing an alarm directly to the Chicago police station half a block away. Our building, we thought, was impregnable.

Marvin's spacious and opulent second-floor office faced west toward LaSalle Street and was now occupied by Anson Isaacson, the managing partner who had replaced Marvin upon his death. Our daily partners meeting was held in Anson's office between 9:00 and 10:00 a.m. Normally, there would be eight or nine partners in Anson's office at 9:55 a.m., but that morning we'd broken up a few minutes early. Only three of us were left in the room: Anson, partner Joe Callan, and me. When the phone rang next to me, I answered and Pauline, the receptionist, told me I had a call from a man named Jim Salem, whom I had talked to a week earlier about our Evel Knievel Stunt Cycle toy.

I wouldn't usually leave a meeting, but that morning I decided to take the phone call in another room. I stepped out through Anson's back door and walked a few steps down the hall into an empty executive's office. If I hadn't moved to a different office to take Jim's call, I would have been murdered that day.

At the same time I started talking to Jim on the phone, a deranged employee climbed up the back stairs, walked down the long corridor, opened the solid back door of Anson's office and walked in. Al Keller, whom I knew only as a quiet electrical engineer, was armed with two handguns. He shot Anson in the face twice, killing him instantly. Keller then shot Joe three times in the chest, killing him. Keller exited through the back door and turned back the way he had come, away from the office where I was talking on the phone. Keller kept shooting as he moved down the hall into the toy designer's space. (See diagram p. **117**.)

I heard only a popping sound when Keller fired his pistol. I didn't recognize the noise and guessed it might be a toy gun. I put Jim on hold and stepped into the hallway to see what was happening. When I noticed the back door to Anson's office was wide open, I walked in. I could not believe what I saw in front of me.

My first thought was that an unknown madman had entered through the front door. It never occurred to me that the shooter was an employee, or that he had entered and exited through the same back door I used. I raced out the front door of the office to our confused receptionist, Pauline, screaming, "Where did he go?" Because of a small elevator in the front hallway that partially separated her desk from Anson's office, Pauline hadn't heard a thing.

Before it was over, Keller murdered three people, grievously injured two more, and then killed himself. The shooting lasted no more than two minutes—two minutes that changed my life and the lives of our employees forever.

I lived only because I answered a phone call. I came within moments of being gunned down by a psychotic madman who was convinced that his coworkers were conspiring to kill him. I have no doubt I was meant to die that day.

After the horrific crime scene was under control, the police homicide commander, Joseph DiLeonardi, found me sitting in shock in the same executive's office where I had taken my life-saving phone call. When the commander asked me who I was, I told him I was a partner. He told me they had searched Keller's body and found several pages of handwritten notes stuffed in his sock. Surprisingly, DiLeonardi handed me two pages of Keller's notes and left the room.

I quickly read the two pages as I sat holding them in my hand. My only thought was to get rid of them, and I decided to burn them in a heavy glass ashtray sitting on the desk. I never wanted to see those terrible papers again. Keller had written down the names of fourteen people he meant to kill that day. As I watched the notes burn to soot in the ashtray, I saw that the second name on the list was mine.

How do you earn a profit from fun? How do you spark creativity? And how do you triumph over unthinkable adversity?

I emerged from my Jewish neighborhood in Chicago in the early 1960s as an imaginative, driven, but failing college student. I was on terminal probation as a freshman at Bradley University in Peoria. I was stuck on "duh" and on the road to nowhere when I took a weekend trip to visit high school friends at the University of Illinois in Urbana-Champaign. While there, I found my purpose in life in one afternoon, during an accidental meeting in a dingy office with a hippie industrial design professor named Ed Zagorski.

As a boy, I had spent countless hours taking apart and examining machines and gadgets. I *had* to know—how does this machine work? What does this part do? Why does this gadget function? Why, why, why? As I talked with Ed Zagorski about industrial design, I realized the subject answered all the questions that fired my imagination. Our brief conversation changed my life. When I walked out of Zagorski's office I had a mission. I was going to transfer to the University of Illinois, become an industrial design major, and take Ed Zagorski's class. I'd found the thing I didn't even know I was looking for.

As a young man, I found my niche in life by designing toys for Marvin Glass & Associates. I combined my competitive work ethic, childlike heart, and fertile imagination to invent classic games that still sell more than fifty years later. I created dozens of games, including Bucket of Fun, Masterpiece, the Trump Game, and Guesstures. I became the only toy designer to win two *Good Housekeeping* awards for inventing the best game of the year—Ants in the Pants in 1969 and Masterpiece in 1970.

I went on to lead two influential and profitable toy design studios for forty-one years, Marvin Glass & Associates and Big Monster Toys. I oversaw the production of hundreds of toys, including Simon, Fashion Polly Pocket, and Uno Attack! During those years we successfully adapted as the toy industry underwent a massive transformation into electronics and computers, echoing the rest of industrial society.

Along the way I enjoyed a happy family life as the devoted father of three sons and four grandsons. I traveled with my wife to the Soviet Union to aid Refuseniks in their plight in 1981. I left the toy industry in 2008 and turned my hand to sculpting in bronze, wood, and stone. I have permanent sculptures on display in Uruguay, Vermont, California, New Jersey, and at the University of Illinois.

For decades, I prospered in an industry that focuses on fun, happiness, and play. My charmed life, however, wasn't always as easy as it seemed.

Chapter 1

Work + Fun = Happy

I started my first business in 1948, when I was five years old. I earned five cents. I was hired for my first job when I was six years old. I earned thirty cents. Then, when I was eight, I started my second business and again earned thirty cents. I loved to work then, and I still love to work now, more than seventy years later.

When I was five, my beloved grandfather Jacob and I built a shoeshine box. We had a wonderful time crafting the wooden box and neatly arranging the shoe polish and brush. The next morning, I got up before the sun and left the house, proudly carrying my homemade equipment and ready to start my career as a shoeshine boy. I decided to charge each customer five cents, which struck me as a fair price. I headed for the CTA train stop two blocks away from where we lived on Chicago's North Side. It felt great to be going to work just like my dad, who was still asleep when I walked out the door.

My first and only customer was Mr. Goldstein, the father of my brother's friend, who lived in an apartment half a block from our house on Kimball Avenue. Mr. Goldstein came up behind me as I hurried to the Lawrence Avenue CTA stop. He refused when I asked him if he wanted a shoeshine and said, "It's too early in the morning and you're too young to go to work." He escorted me home and handed me a nickel as he kindly advised, "Jeffrey, put away your shoeshine box and go back to sleep." I did. That was the end of my first job. Unearned profit: five cents!

I decided to get back to work one year later. I'm not sure how I got hired as a newspaper delivery boy as a six-year-old, but when I showed up at the storefront on Lawrence Avenue with my Red Radio Flyer wagon ready to go, they employed me. "Here's your delivery route," the man told me as he handed me a large steel ring holding many cardboard cards, each displaying the name and address of a customer. Fortunately, I was a good reader for a six-year-old. They loaded up my wagon and I started off, but it was tough pulling the heavy load of newspapers through my neighborhood. The wagon was much too heavy for me. Back then the sidewalks didn't have corner curb ramps, so lifting the loaded wagon up and down the curbs was really hard. I only lasted three days, but this time I earned thirty cents!

Two years later I conceived another business adventure. My family often enjoyed an outing to the specialty grocery store on Devon Avenue, three miles north of us. Happily, my parents allowed my older brother and me to play miniature golf at the nearby course while they shopped. We loved playing on the little holes with their ramps, curves, and unexpected surprises. One day we had so much fun that inspiration seized my eight-year-old brain—I was going back into business!

I decided to build my own miniature golf course. I quickly converted an empty lot next to my house into a three-hole game. I flattened out the dirt and used two-by-fours to make the putting surface. I dug holes and buried empty tin soup cans to create the openings where the golf ball would drop. I charged three cents to play, a penny for each hole. My dad let me borrow three white golf balls, but I wasn't allowed to paint them different colors or add stripes. My customers needed to take turns because my dad only owned one putter. It wasn't much of a golf course, and when it rained everything in the lot turned to mud, but the kids in the neighborhood had a lot of fun while it lasted. I think I made thirty cents!

My first three jobs didn't work out the way I planned, like so much in life. But I learned I loved to work and was good at building things with my hands. I discovered if I combined my imagination and curiosity with my work ethic and construction skills, I could bring my ideas to life. I understood work and business could be fun. Even then, I had the heart of a toy designer.

Ever since I was a little boy, I've wanted to figure out how and why things worked. When I saw a machine or gadget, I yearned to understand the secrets hidden *inside* the casings. I had to know, and the only way to learn was to open them up and examine the interior. I spent hours and hours at my dad's little workbench in the basement, dismantling mechanisms and studying how they functioned.

I grew up in the 1940s and '50s in a Jewish neighborhood called Albany Park, northwest of Wrigley Field and about four miles west of Lake Michigan. I was fortunate to grow up in an unusually loving family, although I didn't realize it until I was older. My parents never swore and neither did we. They lived by the motto, "If you can't say anything nice…." They encouraged us to find our own place in the world and let my brother and me make mistakes. However, they also demanded discipline and expected us to do our chores and earn our allowances.

In 1945, after living in an apartment during the war years, my parents bought a red brick house with a detached two-car garage on the alley. We lived on Kimball Avenue, which was a fairly busy north-south street. We had three little bedrooms and one and a half bathrooms. Our house felt enormous to me. My older brother Gene and I shared one small bedroom because my parents believed sharing was important. I decorated our bedroom by hanging lots of my toy model airplanes from the ceiling using fishing line. When our window was open the planes would go "flying" over our beds.

My mom stayed at home and took care of us. She taught me a crucial lesson when I was a little boy. "Do the best you can with whatever you're doing," she instructed, "no matter what it is." More importantly, that's how she lived. A terrific cook, my mom always had a warm meal ready for my brother and me when we walked home for lunch on school days. My mom encouraged my building projects and inventions, but she expected me to clean up when I was done, and I did.

My dad always built things. If we needed something, we didn't go to Sears. We made it ourselves using hand tools. One of our first family projects was the transformation of part of our garage into a greenhouse. My father was a talented gardener who loved to grow fresh flowers for my mom, particularly dahlias, and he didn't want Chicago's winters interfering with his blooms. We set to work.

My dad and uncle demolished part of the roof and one outside wall, replacing them with glass panels to let in the sunlight. My brother and I pitched in by carrying things here and there. We watched as the dark garage was converted into a sunlit space, an oasis filled with beauty, filled with life. My dad built growing trays and planted seeds that grew into spectacular flowers in all the colors of the rainbow. Proud of my dad's green thumb, I loved his beautiful flowers.

Our next family project was constructing a breakfast room. Our house had an open back porch that my dad decided to enclose with glass blocks. He built the entire structure in one day, and my brother and I helped when we could. My dad, however, wasn't a mason and neglected to let the mortar on the lower blocks set before adding more blocks. From then on, we were delighted to eat our toast and cereal while looking through the crooked glass walls of our hand-built breakfast room.

My father owned and was president of a small textile printing business, R. A. Briggs and Company. The company printed floral designs on white terrycloth bath towels, hand towels, and washcloths. In 1951, when I was eight years old, my father's business partner gave our family a seven-inch black-and-white television set. We were the first family in the neighborhood to own one.

Televisions were so remarkable then that my entire third-grade class came to my house to see it. The newfangled device was a big wooden box with a little seven-inch screen on one side. The first show broadcast locally was a puppet show called *Kukla, Fran, and Ollie*. Watching the puppets on TV was magical. I was fascinated with the machine and wanted to know how it worked. Knowing my predilection for opening up gadgets and tinkering with them, my father warned, "Don't open that up. Don't touch it." I obeyed. After all, I had other diversions to entertain me.

My favorite toy was a wonderful metal construction kit called an Erector Set. When I opened the box, it contained motors, gears, pulleys, screws, nuts, bolts, and lightweight metal beams with holes and slots in them. I could build one moving, whirring contraption, then deconstruct it and immediately create another one. The possibilities were endless—it was incredible!

Highly competitive, I loved to play games against my friends and brother. I loved to play Monopoly, and back then the game came with real wooden houses and hotels. Die-cast metal pieces, including a dog, shoe, and iron, represented each player on the board. I didn't know what the word "monopoly" meant and I didn't care—I just wanted to win. I knew that I needed to acquire all the properties of the same color and the four railroads to have the best chance. None of the names meant anything to me, but I knew that Boardwalk and Park Place were dark blue and if you owned those, you usually won. The dark purple were Mediterranean Avenue and Baltic Avenue, and even at eight years old I knew they were lousy properties and I never bought them.

Playing games gave me confidence and unleashed my imagination. More importantly, it taught me how to lose and come back for more. As much as I wanted to win, I instinctively understood that there was always another game to play. I was a good chess player, but I sought out players who were better than me. I was willing to lose so that I could learn from them. I knew that playing against better players made me a better chess player in the long run. I spent a lot of time playing games, building toys, and making friends.

My older brother Gene, however, thought it was his job to tease me non-stop. I remember one time when I was seven years old chasing him around our small dining room table with a baseball bat, intending to hit him with it as revenge for his teasing, until dad stopped me. He suggested the antidote to Gene's teasing was to ignore him. "If you don't get upset," explained my dad quietly, "there's no sense in what your brother is doing, and he'll stop." It wasn't easy, but I listened, and Gene stopped teasing me a few days later. We've been best friends ever since.

Every Saturday morning, I walked to the Terminal Movie Theater and watched cartoons and a double feature with three of my friends. When the show ended, Paul, Leo, Eddie, and I hurried two blocks to Lerner's Hot Dog Place to eat the best kosher hot dogs in Albany Park. A hot dog and fries were a quarter. The hot dog man pulled the warm, soft bun out of a metal steaming box and tucked the hot dog inside, adding a giant kosher pickle and mustard. Ketchup was not allowed at Lerner's. In Albany Park in the 1940s, you didn't put ketchup on a kosher hot dog. I think it might have been illegal.

Paul was a good pal who lived with his parents above his father's drug store. One of the things we liked to do was play with Lady Fingers, small firecrackers that we got our hands on one Fourth of July holiday. We were so intrigued with the noisy devices that we thought it would be fun to mix our own gunpowder and manufacture our own firecrackers.

My dad was a chemist and gave me a chemistry set as a gift for my ninth birthday, probably to see if I showed interest in his field. The set contained many little glass bottles with different types of powdered chemicals. A small booklet listed chemical formulas, but Paul and I were disappointed to learn there was no recipe for gunpowder. Undaunted, I asked my dad.

"Dad," I asked innocently, "what is gunpowder made from?" He was happy that I was interested in chemistry and promptly replied, "Sulfur, charcoal, and potassium nitrate." He explained the chemicals were mixed at a ratio of three parts to two parts to one part, but he didn't say which chemical was which part. I didn't ask. I guessed he didn't want to reveal too much information.

Paul and I set to work. We calculated there were only six possible combinations, and, of course, opted to manufacture and test them all. My chemistry kit contained bottles of sulfur and charcoal, but potassium nitrate was trickier to obtain because it wasn't sold over the counter. Paul's dad was a pharmacist, and Paul knew that potassium nitrate was commonly known as saltpeter. "I can get some from my dad," promised Paul, and he did, but I never asked how.

Paul and I sat in the hallway outside his apartment and mixed the combination of powders into six little piles. We lit each pile with wooden matches, and one of the piles burned instantly. We were sure we'd made gunpowder, but we could never get our firecrackers to burst. We couldn't get the fuse to burn correctly and we couldn't roll the paper tightly enough to contain the gunpowder, which was probably just as well. We were happy with our experiment. I was sure I could have been a bomb maker.

Growing up in the late '40s and early '50s in crowded cities was a terrifying prospect for one reason: polio. The terrible virus spread easily among children, particularly in summer when kids played in swimming pools and socialized closely together. My parents had dear friends whose oldest son contracted polio. Joel developed a terrible limp and watching him walk was painful.

In the summer of 1950, desperate to protect us from this potentially lethal virus, my parents sent us north to an eight-week summer camp. Gene was nine and I was only seven years old. If polio wasn't running rampant at home, I wouldn't have been sent away at such a young age.

Camp Glen Eden sat on idyllic Anvil Lake near Eagle River, Wisconsin. Eagle River was a summer camp mecca then, a small, rustic town set amidst a vast northern forest. Our primitive camp consisted of eight small wooden cabins facing the pristine lake. My cabin housed five bunk beds, without electricity or heat. We hiked through a growth of trees and up a little hill for the outhouse and showers (cold water only). We ate simple meals served family-style in a mess hall. There were no radios, record players, or television, and just one pay phone in the office to call home. It was wonderful!

During the day we swam, boated, made crafts, and shot bows and arrows. At night, we told ghost stories to scare ourselves to sleep, using flashlights to heighten the suspense and make the scary parts even scarier. I loved telling ghost stories, but my favorite activity was the Saturday night social dance with the girls' camp across Anvil Lake.

One rule was ironclad. Before walking into the dining hall for dinner, each camper had to hand the counselor a postcard addressed to Mom and Dad. When we packed for camp, we made sure to include pre-stamped postcards, which cost one penny to mail in 1950. My missives went more or less like this:

Monday: "Hi mom and dad, miss you. Love Jeffrey"
Tuesday: "Raining today, yea no swimming. Love Jeffrey"
Wednesday: "Had a great day today. Love Jeff"
Thursday: "Send bubble gum. Love J. B."
Friday: "Last card, mail next week. Love me."

Gene and I spent three happy summers at Camp Glen Eden. But going away to overnight camp did more than safeguard me from polio—it helped me grow up. I learned to make my own decisions away from my parents. My dad must have thought I was maturing intellectually as well, because when I was ten or eleven years old, he gave me one of my greatest gifts—my own real slot machine to decipher.

Across the street from my dad's factory in the early '50s stood a tavern that boasted nickel slot machines. One night the owner of the bar told my dad that the police were clamping down on gambling and that his nickel slot machines had to go. My dad bought one for twenty-five dollars and brought it home for me when I was ten years old. I had no idea what it was.

My dad explained that people gambled with slot machines—they put money in the coin slot on top, pulled the mechanical arm all the way down, and watched as the three wheels spun. After the wheels stopped, most of the time nothing happened. "You just lost your nickel and often all of your money," Dad said. "You might win a few coins back, and you might even win the jackpot, but that's rare." He told me that's why it's also called a "one-armed bandit." Dad explained that gambling could become addictive. That was a new word for me, and I immediately used "addictive" to describe my dad's smoking habit. I don't think my dad was happy he added that word to my vocabulary.

Dad allowed me to open up the slot machine, but I had to promise not to dismantle it. I felt like a surgeon standing over a patient on the operating table when I placed the three-foot-high machine on my dad's workbench. I used a screwdriver to free the outside casing, then I carefully removed it so that the inside mechanism lay exposed on the workbench. When I saw it, I was amazed. It looked like a gigantic magical toy. I *had* to know how it worked—*how* did the machine know what to do with the nickel?

I was captivated by the idea that one pull of the mechanical arm set wheels spinning, springs coiling, and levers engaging. How did one pull cause all this movement? How did it create random results? I had to know. In order to puzzle out its movements, I had to think critically about how and why it functioned. Why was this lever here? Why was that spring there? What caused this wheel to spin and that pin to activate? That was the fascinating wonder of it.

When I dropped the coin and pulled the arm, the machine knew what to do. If a particular pattern of cherries and bars came up, it paid out a few nickels. If three bars in a row came up, it emptied the whole container—jackpot! I studied this fascinating puzzle for hours, pulling the arm repeatedly and observing where every spring coiled and every lever and rod clicked into place.

Without using tools, I learned how to manipulate the mechanism so that it hit the jackpot every time. I saw that pulling the arm down activated springs and started the three wheels spinning. The wheels displayed the bars and cherries. I discovered I could pause the mechanism after pulling down the arm if I grabbed onto one of the gears with one hand. I used my other hand to manually turn the three wheels to display three bars, which signified the jackpot. When I released the gear, the machine went back to work and small rods shifted into place, and...*presto!* The machine showed jackpot. Even better, I figured it out without ruining the machine. I felt like I had found the treasure where *X* marks the spot!

Chapter 2

Finding What I Didn't Even Know I Was Looking For

I think I got my talent for invention from my paternal grandfather, Jacob, who had emigrated alone from Kiev, Russia, as a penniless seventeen-year-old. He loved to fish, and he often took my brother and me to Lake Michigan to catch perch. We fished off high concrete piers that jutted out into the deep blue water. On nice days there would be dozens of fishermen angling for perch.

Grandpa explained that fish travel in schools, and if one perch grabs a worm and gets hooked, there's nothing left for the others. So just like my father, who built what he needed, Grandpa built a fishing contraption with six hooks and six worms attached to the line to tantalize all the fish. There was a little bell attached to the top of the line that chimed when we caught a fish. I asked Grandpa why they call them schools, because the fish never seem to learn how not to get caught. He smiled but offered no answer.

We sat for hours on little stools, drinking Dr. Pepper, reading the paper, and listening for the bell to ring. We knew we caught a fish when the bell chimed, *ding, ding, ding*. Grandpa let us pull up the line and we always saw at least one fish and sometimes more. Since then, I've fished all over North America with my friends and family, but no happy memory comes close to those warm summer days sitting on a stool, sipping Dr. Pepper with my grandpa, waiting to hear the soft peal of the *ding, ding, ding*.

As I got older, I started building my own inventions. One of my devices got me in trouble. I was on the Patrol Squad when I was in seventh grade. Patrols helped the grammar school kids cross the busy street. It was an honor to be selected and I was proud to be part of the squad. Drivers could distinguish us because we wore a cool white belt that wrapped around our waist and crossed over our shoulder.

Billy Jacobs sat next to me in class. He was a big kid with red curly hair and lots of freckles. One day I decided to play a practical joke on my friend. Underneath our school desks was a wide slot with an opening where we stored books and supplies. I rigged Billy's desk one day during recess when the classroom was empty. I placed a small tin container filled with water into the wide slot's opening. I taped a piece of thread to the front of the tin, ran it around the bottom of the desk, and taped the thread to the bottom of the book on his desk.

When Billy returned from recess, I told him he needed to look at an assignment in his book. He lifted up his book, the tin container dumped water right in his crotch, and he screamed and jumped out of his seat. My mechanism had worked perfectly! Billy and I stayed friends, but the teacher didn't think it was funny. I got kicked off the Patrol Squad and lost my cool white belt.

When I was sixteen years old, I worked in my dad's warehouse for the summer, packing and shipping finished products. I was glad to be earning the minimum wage of $1.25 an hour. My dad ran his company from his office. I didn't see him all day as I labored in the factory, but on Fridays we ate lunch together. By summer's end, I knew I didn't want to work for my dad. I realized I needed to find my own path. I'm grateful my dad never made me feel my future was tied to his business. I worked all through college, and a strong work ethic has stayed with me all of my life.

In elementary school I had skipped a year, jumping from third to fifth grade, so I was young when I started high school in the late 1950s. I felt different than the other kids because of that one-year age gap. On top of that, my parents decided to build a new house in Skokie, a suburb just north of Chicago. The house wouldn't be completed for months, but my dad arranged for me to start my freshman year at Niles Township High School in Skokie. Unlike my brother, who had walked one block to our neighborhood high school, as a freshman I needed to take two buses to get to and from school each day. These changes led to one result—I was a lousy student.

I disliked history and hated trigonometry. Lazy and unmotivated, I never got a grade higher than a C, except for a B in gym and an A in art. But what an A it was—it changed my life. Hazel Loew taught art class in my sophomore year. She was a short, elf-like inspiration and a joy to be around. Hazel showed me that art was fun and helped me discover that I was a good artist. For one of her assignments, I carved an abstract figure of a woman out of a block of mahogany. The abstract woman is eleven inches tall, stands on a two-inch cube base, and sits on my desk to this day.

Hazel became my first mentor. It was she who gave me the confidence to pursue art as a profession. Without her, I never would have walked into the art building on the University of Illinois campus three years later, finding my career path in the process. I've led a prosperous, charmed life because Hazel Loew, my high school art teacher, believed in me.

But when I graduated from high school in 1960, no one foresaw my bright future, least of all me. I ranked in the bottom 25 percent of my class. My high school counselor suggested I go to Bradley University in Peoria because she thought I couldn't hack it at the University of Illinois. When I arrived at Bradley that fall, my unfocused brain was stuck on "duh."

At Bradley, I majored in drinking and minored in partying. I lost my virginity, learned to drink, and failed my classes, not necessarily in that order. I was on terminal probation after my first semester. With no idea what to do or where to go, I was firmly on the road to nowhere.

During second semester, I thought a road trip would help me clear my head. My friend Rick let me borrow his car—a VW Beetle with a stick shift. If I hadn't known how to drive a stick shift, my life would be completely different today. One spring weekend in 1961 I drove ninety miles in a snowstorm across flat, open farmland to party with friends at the University of Illinois in Urbana-Champaign. My life was never the same.

I got to the U. of I. early on that Friday and had time to kill that afternoon while I waited for my friends to get out of class. I wandered around campus and walked into the newly rebuilt Fine Arts Building. I walked down the hallway where a dazzling display inside a glass cabinet caught my eye. Inside the glass case I saw a spectacular exhibit of brilliantly colored and uniquely designed wooden blocks. I was captivated at that moment.

The exhibit was titled the "Three Cut Project" and was created by industrial design students. I had never heard of industrial design, but in those eye-catching wooden blocks I sensed possibilities for my future. A card explained that each student was given a block of soft pine wood, about twelve inches long and about twice as high and wide as a stick of butter. The students were assigned to use a band saw to cut the wood into four pieces, making the three cuts wherever they wanted. They glued the four pieces back together to make a unique design of their choosing, then carefully sanded down the resulting wood sculpture. Finally, they used a high-quality sprayer to paint their piece in different colors of shiny automotive paint. The results were stunning. The instructor's name was on the card—Ed Zagorski.

When I finally tore myself away from the display, I saw a faculty office with its door ajar. One of the names on the glass was Edward Zagorski. I knocked and went in, not knowing what to say or even why I was there. But the only man in the room was sitting at a desk and made me feel at ease. I liked him before he even said hello. He was near forty and was dressed in jeans, T-shirt, and sandals. He was over six feet tall, with uncombed hair and horn-rimmed glasses. This was Ed Zagorski.

I told Zagorski I was fascinated by his "Three Cut Project" and asked him to tell me about it. For twenty minutes he enthusiastically explained how industrial design was the secret operator behind everything: automobiles, furniture, appliances, telephones, and tools. Zagorski believed deeply that a design has to work first, then look great. He was likable, childlike, and uninhibited in his passion for design.

As Professor Zagorski talked, a light went on in my head—this is what I was born to do! I realized that industrial design answered all of the questions that fired my imagination as a boy: How does this work? What does this do? Why does this work? I had been desperate to know the answers to these questions as a little boy, and in his classroom I could finally learn all the answers.

Our brief conversation changed my life. I'd always had intelligence and ability, but I'd lacked ambition to do anything with it. But when I walked out of Ed Zagorski's office, I had a mission. I was going to transfer to the University of Illinois, become an industrial design major, and take Ed Zagorski's class. I'd found the thing I didn't even know I was looking for.

I returned to Bradley highly motivated. I improved my grades and made the dean's list, and then I transferred to Illinois beginning in the winter semester of 1962. My credits didn't transfer from Bradley, but I didn't care. As a freshman at the U. of I., I had a new ID card and a clear-cut goal in my sights.

In the early 1960s, all male students at Bradley and the U. of I. were required to take two years of Reserve Officer Training Corps (ROTC). I disliked ROTC and was one semester short when I transferred, but

Bradley mistakenly told Illinois I had fulfilled my two-year requirement. I didn't tell the U. of I. that Bradley had gotten it wrong. I was delighted to be done with wearing itchy wool uniforms and marching with a rifle.

As a freshman, I started with basic classes in design, drawing, and art history, subjects that I had barely touched until now. It was at the beginning of my art history class that two men, Michelangelo and Leonardo da Vinci, sparked my intense and lifelong love affair with art. I couldn't get enough of their work—their five-hundred-year-old genius grabbed me and wouldn't let me go. Later in the year we studied the French Impressionists, and I can still recognize the works of Van Gogh, Renoir, Monet, Manet, Gauguin, Cezanne, and more. My favorite sculptor of that period was Auguste Rodin, whose bronze figures are breathtaking. It was my art history course that opened up the vibrant world where I have happily spent the rest of my life.

Outside of class, I joined a fraternity, Alpha Epsilon Pi. I had a few high school friends in AEP, and as a pledge I lived in the old fraternity house while a new one was under construction. I survived hell week and got a fraternity pin, learned the secret handshake, and was inducted in a midnight ceremony. I felt like Greek life was a mini cult. I played sports for my frat, including intramural tennis and table tennis, and my social life revolved around Greek parties and dances. I also loved going to football games and cheering for Dick Butkus, our Hall of Fame linebacker. I worked at various jobs, but my favorite was waiting tables at Thunderbird Pizza. It was fun and I could always eat free pizza when I wasn't working.

A basic shop course called Materials and Process was required for every sophomore industrial design student. There we learned about the nuts and bolts of tools and machinery—different woods, plastics, metals, and model making. We acquired the skills to manipulate and mold materials with hand tools and shop machines, including a lathe, milling machine, and drill press. Several different electric saws and sanders stood in the room, each with a specific purpose. The U. of I. boasted a fully equipped and impressive machine shop.

Leonard Price was our instructor, and he supervised the workshop. He rubbed us the wrong way with his strict shop rules, and students constantly made fun of him. As far as we knew, Leonard's life consisted of two things: teaching shop and doting on his fancy white 1960 Porsche Abarth 356B Carrera GTL. I've never cared about cars. Leonard, on the other hand, kept his Porsche and his workshop spotless. Nerdiness aside, however, Leonard was a smart and savvy instructor who made sure we understood shop safety.

Leonard taught us that each machine and tool is designed for a specific job: a table saw is used for crosscutting and ripping, a hack saw is used for metal, and a miter saw is used for cutting angles for trim. The list goes on. Leonard instructed us to respect each tool or machine and to use it only for its purpose.

In the middle of the semester an opening came up for a nighttime shop attendant. I needed the money and took the job, which meant that Leonard became my boss in addition to my instructor. My duties were simple: keep the shop sparkling clean, get everyone out by 9:30 p.m., and lock up.

One night, before Leonard left for the evening, he asked me to paint one of the machines in the shop. He showed me the quart can of gray paint and left. I was alone. I opened the can to find the paint was ancient and thick. I thought it would take forever to mix the old paint by hand with a wooden stick, and, being creative, I came up with an alternate plan. I decided to manufacture my own metal paint-mixer attachment. Then I would insert the attachment into the drill press and let the press do the work of mixing the paint—genius!

A drill press is, basically, a motorized machine that works as a much faster and more powerful handheld drill. It's designed to bore holes in wood, metal, or plastic, and the piece being drilled is usually clamped into a vise resting on a table.

I found a thin steel rod about ten inches long. I secured it in the vise and tightened it, leaving one inch sticking out of the jaws. With a hammer, I pounded the one-inch portion sideways until it was bent ninety degrees. *Presto!* I had created my own metal paint mixer that I could insert into the drill press.

A Game Maker's Life

I placed the open paint can on the drill press table and positioned it so that my little L was now inside the thick gray paint. I was ready to go, but instead of clamping the paint can into a vise, for some reason I thought it would be a good idea to hold the can in one hand. I pushed the start button on the drill press and all hell broke loose.

Instantly, the powerful drill press ripped the can out of my hand. Gray paint shot all over the room. The can caught on the metal attachment and spun around like crazy, spraying paint everywhere. I panicked and couldn't hit the off button fast enough. By the time the can stopped spinning the shop looked like a Jackson Pollack painting done entirely in gray. I was doomed.

Wet paint dripped slowly in every nook and cranny—on the walls, machinery, floor, ceiling, and even on the high windows along the far wall. The only thing I had done right was wear my goggles. It took me an hour just to clean the paint off my face, neck, and hands. I didn't even try to clean the shop that night. By the time I got back to my frat house I couldn't wait to get out of my paint-splattered clothes so my brothers would stop staring at me and laughing. It was a long and brutal evening.

Scared shitless at what I had done to Leonard's pristine workshop, I had neglected his cardinal rule: "Don't use a machine or tool for a job it was not designed for." I had ignored the fact that a drill press is not a paint mixer. The next morning, I got to the building early and stopped Leonard before he walked into the shop. I tried to explain what I had done, but it didn't work. When I opened the door, I faced a disaster. It looked much worse than I remembered from the night before. Leonard went ballistic. I thought he was going to slug me, but he didn't. I learned my lesson, though—I never again misused a machine tool.

I lost my job as the shop attendant. I worked every evening for two weeks to clean the shop. I was the laughingstock of the entire Fine Arts Building. My classmates told everyone to come see my masterpiece in the shop. My new nickname was Jackson. The ridicule pained me and I couldn't laugh about it until after I had graduated from college and built a successful career.

17

Chapter 3

Learning *How* to Think

F reshman year at the U. of I. flew by, and when sophomore year started, I couldn't wait to take Ed Zagorski's industrial design class. I had transformed my life in order to reach my goal, which was taking this class. Instead of carrying on living the life of a drunken party boy at Bradley University, I had forced myself to study and make the dean's list. I had grown into a young man by the time I transferred to the University of Illinois. When I walked into Ed's class on the first day, I was excited and nervous, hoping it wouldn't be a disappointment. Happily, it exceeded expectations beyond my wildest dreams. Zagorski's industrial design class changed me. Ed altered how I thought about and looked at the world. Best of all, Ed became a lifelong friend and my second mentor.

Zagorski taught us *how* to solve problems. He focused our minds on developing our creative thinking. Zagorski's assignments were designed to make us think about how we should explore a problem rather than the ultimate solution. Looking at a problem from multiple perspectives and asking the right questions are skills that have stayed with me. My career as a toy designer was strongly influenced by five of Ed's most memorable assignments.

The first assignment came when one day Ed pulled out a coin, shouted to us to "call it out" and flipped it in the air. Half of us yelled heads and the rest tails. "A coin," Ed explained simply, "is a random decision maker." Then he pulled out a single die and rolled it, showing us a different decision maker. "A random choice, but this time it's one of six," he said. His last example was a little dreidel, a four-sided Jewish variant on a teetotum, which is a random decision maker found in many ancient European countries. Ed spun the top, and after a few seconds it stopped and, totally by chance, landed on one of its four sides. This led to our next task. We had to create and build our *own* random decision maker, something that had never been done before. The object we designed could have as many sides as we wanted, but it had to randomly land on one side.

I spent the next two weeks solving this seemingly simple problem. My solution resembled a short, blocky flying pencil. I carved a rectangular piece of wood, similar to a four-sided pencil, about five inches long and about one inch high by one inch wide. I labeled each of the sides with a number, one through four. Then I carved both ends to a soft point. I took a separate wooden rod and tapped down on one of the pointed ends, which flipped the rectangular piece up in the air. It jumped about a foot off the table and landed, at random, on one of the numbered sides. It wasn't the best design in the class, but it wasn't the worst.

I became a minor celebrity in my frat house because of Zagorski and his class projects. My Greek brothers always hung out in my room, wanting to see what I was working on. No one waited around to see what the students majoring in history or accounting were up to, but my fascinating projects made me the center of attention. I learned early on that my field of industrial design was unknown to most people. I was lucky to be creative and have fun at school.

The second project was to create a Rube Goldberg type of machine. Rube Goldberg was an American cartoonist and inventor who drew complicated devices to complete simple tasks. Ed's assignment was to build our own Rube Goldberg device that would fit into a cubic foot of space (that's twelve inches by twelve inches by twelve inches). We were each given an identical steel ball bearing that measured half an inch in diameter.

The goal was to release the ball somewhere near the top of your device and keep the ball in motion for as long as possible. It should only come to a stop because of gravity and friction. We were not allowed to use any electrical power, battery, or small motor. You could not wind up a spring that would somehow add energy to the ball inside your cube. Grades were based only on the result—the longer your ball stayed in motion, the higher your grade.

The Mouse Trap game that was designed by Marvin Glass & Associates and manufactured by Ideal Toy Company in the early '60s was basically a Rube Goldberg machine. At the time, however, I was aware of neither Mouse Trap nor Marvin Glass & Associates (MGA). The Zagorski cubic-foot Rube Goldberg "mousetrap" solutions were spectacular, and many of my classmates' balls stayed in motion for over sixty seconds, although mine didn't. My project was ranked in the middle of the class.

Creating something was half the fun of Ed's projects; the other half was seeing the results from everyone else in the class. One of the advantages of being in class was the interaction between students. Everyone helped each other, and if you had a suggestion that you thought would make an improvement to another classmate's project, you freely offered it. Zagorski impressed upon all of us that we were on the same team, even if we were designing different products. This fundamental lesson in cooperation was to prove essential in my career as a toy designer.

The third assignment was designed to increase our awareness of our sense of touch and its importance in good design. We were to carve a design, anything we wanted, out of a block of hardwood, about six inches on each side, or about the size of a small melon. Our project would be graded by three outside instructors, who would be blindfolded and judge our work only on how it felt to them. We were given a choice of maple, walnut, or mahogany wood. Maple and walnut are predominantly North American woods. Mahogany trees grow in tropical forests in South

America and Africa. I chose mahogany, because I wanted my solution to be exotic and come from a place I had never visited.

As I carefully carved the gorgeous, amber-colored wood, I often took breaks so I could close my eyes and feel the wood taking shape beneath my fingers. I noted how every flick of my knife created new curves, bumps, and ridges in my abstract figure. I meticulously sanded and varnished my figure, and when finished, my sculpture resembled a twisted toy balloon dog and felt flawlessly smooth. Part of our assignment was also to judge other students' work with our eyes closed. I was fascinated to discover that what looked fabulous usually also felt fabulous.

When the day came, we handed our sculpture to the first blindfolded instructor, who felt it for as long as he liked. He then showed his grade by holding up one to ten fingers so the other instructors wouldn't know how he had scored the project. My grade was in the top quarter of the class, and I was delighted that things were moving in the right direction.

The fourth project was a Zagorski stroke of genius. My class happened to be lucky enough to be the first to get this assignment. The big news in the early '60s was about Yuri Gagarin, the Russian cosmonaut who was the first to successfully orbit the Earth on April 12, 1961. The U.S. sent Alan Shepard into space on May 5 of the same year, beginning the space race with the Soviets. Ed's idea was for each of us to design and build our own space capsule, complete with astronaut, which we would launch and then land on water with our astronaut—hopefully—intact.

Our "astronaut" was a raw chicken egg that we housed inside a space capsule of our own design and construction. Our class built a powerful catapult made from a large flat truck spring that was mounted on a steel base with a latch and release mechanism. Each student loaded his uniquely built capsule onto the catapult and launched it, sending it flying so that it landed far out in the reflection pond in front of the Fine Arts Building. After the capsule was pulled out of the "ocean," a propane torch blasted it for thirty seconds to simulate the heat that a real satellite encounters while entering the earth's atmosphere.

After the heat test we opened our capsule to see if our egg was intact. If it was, we cracked it open to show the egg was raw and prove we hadn't illegally hard-boiled our astronaut ahead of time. All of the eggs that were intact passed the cracking test. If an egg was broken, well, that student's astronaut "died" in flight or during reentry.

I built my space capsule out of two aluminum hard hats used by construction workers. I thought that if they could protect workers' heads, they could protect my astronaut. I filled the hard hats with expanded foam and rubber and other packing materials, placed my egg inside, then bolted the brims of the hats together. Success! My egg-ronaut lived!

Ed was so excited about the project that he contacted *Life* magazine. Their top photographer, Art Shey, came to Champaign to record the dynamic space launch. The Zagorski design project was published in *Life* on April 12, 1963. A young Professor Zagorski, his students, and their space capsules covered a number of pages.

The fifth task launched me directly into my career as a toy designer. We were assigned to design and build an original toy, which sounds simple but isn't. I spent a week sketching ideas to clarify my thinking. What came to me was a variation on the "Three Cut Project" I had seen in the glass cabinet in the hallway two years before. I designed a modular wooden furniture set for preschoolers that consisted of four brightly painted cubes. Depending on how a person arranged them, the colorful cubes could be turned into different pieces of furniture—a children's desk, easel, table, and/or stool.

When Zagorski told me I had received the second-highest grade on the toy design project, I was overjoyed. I had been waiting for this moment since kindergarten. It was the pinnacle of my scholastic achievements. I was great at taking things apart, but to actually create something original filled me with a joyful sense of accomplishment. When I created the children's furniture set, I discovered an inner talent I didn't know existed. I was so excited that I couldn't wait to finish college, and I decided to take extra classes and graduate in three years, by January of 1965.

The project that got the top grade on the toy design project, however, went on to become famous as one of the highest-grossing games in history: Operation. My classmate, John Spinello, designed a game in a rectangular blue metal box, a bit smaller than a breadbasket. Inside the metal box were a buzzer, a battery, a thin metal rod, and two aluminum plates separated by a little space. When you opened the box, you saw the top aluminum plate, which was cut with small holes of various sizes and squiggly zigzag slots. The top plate was connected to the buzzer and to the negative side of the battery. The bottom plate was solid and connected to the positive side of the battery.

The person playing the game picked up the thin metal rod and tried to guide it through a hole or along the zigzag slots without touching the side. If you touched the side of the holes or the zigzag with the metal rod, you completed the battery circuit and would be penalized with a buzzing bell and a spark that made you jump. It was great fun and always got a laugh. John's invention was brilliant.

John was from Chicago and had served in the military before college. His father owned a trucking garage and John knew a lot about mechanics and electricity. John and I were friends and I asked, "What are you going to do with that thing? That's fantastic!" He replied, "My godfather in Chicago works for somebody named Marvin Glass," and when I asked what they did, he said, "It's a toy design company." I'd never heard of a toy design company. It turned out that John's godfather, Sam Cottone, was a model maker for Marvin Glass, the premier toy design company in the world. They licensed their toys and game ideas to Ideal Toy, Milton Bradley, and other leading companies. John told me he intended to use his buzzer box as part of his portfolio when he tried to get a job with MGA.

John Spinello graduated before I did and interviewed with Marvin Glass. Marvin offered John a payment of $500 for the blue metal box, which at that time was more money than one semester's tuition at the University of Illinois. John accepted Marvin's offer, but he never forgave himself for the outright sale of his box. To make matters worse, Marvin didn't offer John a job.

Marvin Glass took John's prototype, improved upon it, and licensed the idea to Milton Bradley. It was designers working for Milton Bradley who came up with the idea to turn the simple metal box into the shape of a human body with a big red nose, and they introduced Operation in

1965. The game has earned many millions of dollars and still sells well today. Many years later, I hired John at MGA and he finally had his chance to work as a toy designer.

Zagorski's toy design project came at the end of my sophomore year, but I was so fascinated with the Marvin Glass toy company that I couldn't stop thinking about it. I was determined to find out everything I could about Marvin Glass, the man who ran the toy design studio in Chicago. It was fantastic that someone in Chicago, my hometown, designed toys as a profession!

It was a bitter-cold day when I walked a mile in a blustering wind to the library, but I just had to learn more about this man. I had to know how to get a job with this guy. I didn't know if anything was written about Glass, but I had a wild hunch there might be. I wasn't studying journalism, but a guy who made a living as a toy designer seemed like a great subject for an article. It took me the entire evening, but I finally found a few articles on Marvin—without the internet or Google, just magazine articles.

The story that I read repeatedly, almost until the library was closing, was from the *Saturday Evening Post*, March 5, 1960, by Peter Wyden. I was still in high school when the article was published. The long story had lots of photographs and was titled "Troubled King of Toys." As I read, my jaw dropped further and further. I finished reading in shock. I read the article again to be sure I had it right. I walked away thinking this guy Marvin Glass was a nut case, paranoid, schizophrenic, a madman, psychotic, obsessed with money, depressed, insanely imaginative, self-destructive, eternally optimistic, and a fuckin' genius. That was the incredible moment when I realized that my goal in life was to invent toys and games for Marvin Glass.

In college, I was good at several things—designing new inventions, shooting pool, and playing ping-pong. And while I learned the practical tools of industrial design in class, I learned one of my most valuable lessons at the ping-pong table. In my last semester, I found myself in a ping-pong tournament. It was a bracket tournament, and I won several rounds.

In one of the final rounds, a graduate student named Ling called me up and we arranged for him to come over and play in my dorm. We set a date and met in the basement where the ping-pong table was located. I had just come from studying and was wearing a pair of jeans and a T-shirt. My opponent arrived, gym bag in hand. He looked the table over like he was buying it, and said, "Do you mind if I change the net?" I said, "OK." I'm thinking, *Is there something wrong with the net?*

Ling took his own net out of his gym bag and put it on the table. Then he removed his jeans, revealing a pair of gym shorts. Next, he pulled out a five-ply ping-pong paddle from his bag. Most paddles were two-ply, including the one I used. I had never seen a five-ply paddle before. It was fitted in a little wood press so it wouldn't warp, just like they applied to wooden tennis rackets in the '50s. Ling undid his paddle from the wood press and started to stretch like he was a gymnast. I wanted to scream, "Let's play some fucking ping-pong, I'm going to beat your ass." After a few more minutes standing around watching him warm up, we finally played.

I lost before we started. Ling was a better player than I, but I could have given him a run for his money if he hadn't psyched me out. Instead, he killed me. Ling undermined my confidence in such a methodical way that I was toast before we ever hit the ball. He came to the match with the sole intention of screwing with my brain before we even started playing, and he did a superb job of it. I learned a crucial life lesson: presentation can make a difference between yes and no, success and failure.

During my last semester in Champaign, I worked on dreaming up new inventions that I hoped would earn a lot of money if I could patent them. I already understood that patents were the key to earning money for an inventor. Outside of class I came up with some non-toy ideas that I thought were original. Like all young inventors, I thought my concepts were unique and I was going to earn millions of dollars—ha! I drew up several designs, but when I conducted a search, I found similar products were already patented. I was so sure one of my ideas was original, however, that I built a prototype.

All laundry detergents were powder at that time. I invented a plastic measuring device with sharp prongs at the end that could be easily inserted into the top of the cardboard detergent box. When you turned the box over the top of the washing machine, the plastic device would portion out the exact amount of detergent needed for one load of clothes. I conducted a patent search and found that several of these inventions were patented between 1920 and 1940. Blast! I learned the valuable lesson that original ideas aren't easy to generate. It prepared me for a lifelong string of rejection after rejection that is an intrinsic part of the invention process.

I finished college in three years and graduated early from the University of Illinois, in January 1965. I moved back to Chicago with a lot of plans. I was twenty-two years old and had my heart set on getting a job with Marvin Glass. I was engaged to my high school sweetheart. I was bursting with hopes and dreams, but could I make them come true?

Chapter 4

"Let's See What You Have"

graduated with the goal of working for Marvin Glass & Associates as a toy designer. I called to arrange an appointment and finally reached an operator, but she told me they weren't granting interviews, much less hiring. I waited a week and called again with the same result. I wasn't going to give up, but in the meantime, I needed to find a job.

I searched the *Chicago Sun-Times* and *Chicago Tribune* want ads and saw that American Hospital Supply Corporation (AHSC) was looking for an industrial designer. AHSC was located in Evanston, a suburb just north of Chicago. I arranged for an interview, got dressed in a suit and tie, and walked in with my portfolio in hand. I was relieved when they invited me back for a second interview. When they offered me $5,200 a year to design medical equipment, I happily accepted the job and started immediately.

My fiancée, Marlene Andalman, had attended Illinois State University when I was at Bradley, but we both transferred to the University of Illinois. Marlene had graduated from college the previous June and was teaching art at a junior high school in Skokie, a suburb west of Evanston. Our wedding date was February 13, 1965, and even though I had just started my job, AHSC allowed me to take a week off for our honeymoon in Jamaica.

Marlene earned $5,600 a year teaching art, so together we enjoyed a nice income of more than $10,000 a year. My dad was always conservative and cautious with money. My brother was similar, but I was, typically, the opposite. I always liked to spend the money I earned. My brother got married two months before I did, and he and his wife, Gillian, rented a two-bedroom, two-bath, third-floor walk-up apartment in an ancient building on the north side of Chicago for $95 a month. The first floor was one floor above ground level, so it was a hike up to their rooms. On the other hand, Marlene and I rented a new one-bedroom, one-bath apartment on Howard Street in Evanston in an elevator building for $135 a month. My dad lectured me that I was throwing away $40 a month for a smaller space, but "What's the matter with you?" was as strong as his reprimand would get.

My life was moving quickly. At twenty-two, I enjoyed a new wife, job, apartment, and car. For the time being, I had to give up on my hopes of being a professional toy designer. Things were great, but who was I kidding? I knew letting go of my dream of designing toys wouldn't be easy. In fact, it was impossible.

My job at American Hospital Supply was designing medical products. I was thrilled I had a good job, but now that I was out of college, I was fair game to be drafted for the Vietnam War. I hated the U.S. involvement in the war and planned to move to Canada if I was drafted. Happily, it turned out AHSC was developing a prototype of a small mobile emergency hospital for the military. It was designed so that a helicopter could lower it anywhere to support wounded soldiers. I wasn't involved on the military hospital project, but my boss and his boss wrote to the draft board telling them I was working on it and, therefore, an important part of the war effort. I ended up getting a two-year draft deferment and was overjoyed my bosses went to bat on my behalf and kept me out of the war.

My day-to-day job consisted of graphic design and market research projects at Evanston Hospital. I worked on hospital research for a month and became friendly with the head nurse of the operating rooms. One day she asked me if I'd like to observe a surgery, and I jumped at the chance even though I was nervous. I dressed in scrubs and a mask and a funny little operating hat. My nurse friend escorted me to the operating room where there were two doctors and many nurses. She told me to stand on a little box about a foot off the ground right next to one of the surgeons so I would get a great view. I stepped up, looked down, and was amazed.

Watching the doctor open the patient's belly and set to work was like opening up the nickel slot machine so I could observe what happened to the coins. This was like *Dr. Kildare* or *Ben Casey*, two medical TV shows my mom liked in the early '60s, except this was real and live. The surgery, done in about two hours, was quite a show for a twenty-two-year-old industrial designer. As I followed the surgeon, I kept thinking of John Spinello's blue box that became Operation. The patient in the operating room didn't have a big red nose that buzzed when the doctors made a mistake. I guess they never did.

One thing I noticed at the hospital was that most of the blood and saline were contained in glass bottles. Plastic bags for the operating room were invented in the '50s, but the hospital still used some glass bottles. I was looking at the plastic IV bags when I suddenly came up with an idea for a new type of blood bag. After getting the OK from my boss to experiment with the idea, I started building a prototype.

The seed of my idea came from a product that came out in the mid '50s called Jiffy Pop popcorn. Jiffy Pop had an animated commercial with music that was akin to today's rap. The product was a disposable popcorn-filled aluminum frying pan with a handle and a top cover made of twisted, lightweight aluminum foil. The aluminum cover lay flat in the pan. When the pan was heated on top of a stove, the popping corn puffed up and the twisted aluminum foil gradually expanded into a giant metal ball filled with popped corn.

My plastic blood bag invention was based on the same principle, except that my empty bag would expand with blood instead of popcorn. I used an empty plastic bag and added two round plastic caps, about one inch in diameter, one for the top and one for the bottom. I drilled a hole and inserted a thin vinyl tube through the top cap. I added a plastic valve that could be opened and closed to prevent air from entering the bag. I used water instead of blood to test the device. I opened the top valve and dripped water through the tube and into the bag. The flat, twisted bag slowly untwisted as the water filled it, just like the Jiffy Pop popcorn bag. Success!

My boss was excited about my idea, and before I knew it, I was on a plane to Los Angeles to present it to the executives in charge of making blood bags. I was thrilled to fly to California by myself to show off my prototype invention, even though nothing came of my design. It was a pivotal moment for me though, because I started to think of myself as more than just a designer—I was also an inventor.

I liked my job, but I spent most of my free time dreaming of designing toys for Marvin Glass. I worked at AHSC for a little over two years and received one salary increase to $5,500 a year. I thought I was doing a good job, but we didn't win the contract for the military field hospital and AHSC could no longer help me with my draft deferment. On the day my deferment expired, my boss called me into a small conference room, handed me a two-week paycheck and told me to pack up my stuff. Without giving me a reason, he told me I was "terminated," not fired. I don't know why.

Heartbroken, embarrassed, and ashamed, I didn't tell anyone I'd been fired. I couldn't bring myself to say that word. I told everyone I'd quit because AHSC could no longer give me a draft deferment and I wanted to try to get a job as a toy designer. My story about quitting instead of being fired stayed with me most of my life, until I began believing it wasn't a lie. I'm glad to finally put it on record that I was fired from my first full-time job, and it was the best thing that ever happened to me.

I had frequently called Marvin Glass & Associates during the previous two years, hoping for an interview, but the woman always replied, "Not hiring, no need to even come in." Every free moment, I had worked on preparing my portfolio in the hope that I would get an interview. Now desperate for a job, I called again and, unbelievably, this time the woman's answer was different—MGA was hiring. My interview was scheduled for 10:00 a.m. on Tuesday, April 11, 1967. Two months shy of my twenty-fourth birthday, my two-year long dream was about to become reality.

Marvin Glass invented the business of independent toy design in the late 1950s, but time and again he lost money when he tried to manufacture the toys himself. Finally, he realized he was good at inventing toys and games, but not good at mass-producing them. Then he had a stroke of genius. Marvin decided to let someone else take the financial risk of manufacturing a million toys. Instead, he would demand that manufacturers pay him a royalty for the one thing he did exceptionally well—invent original toys and games. At that time, royalty payments were common in the publishing and music business, but not in the toy industry.

Marvin Glass was the first independent toy designer to demand royalties and get them. He was able to disrupt the existing business model of an entire industry for two reasons—he repeatedly designed wildly popular toys and he possessed an iron will. Marvin built an empire with his "new" business model because he was brilliant and tenacious enough to copy the idea from other businesses. Marvin Glass was the only man I wanted to work for. Now I had my chance.

A portfolio is an industrial designer's most important representation of college. Grades and recommendations are valuable, but they're overshadowed by your design talents and rendering skills. Unique projects that demonstrate creative thinking are the essence of a good designer. My portfolio included photographs of a small train model I built out of wood, several games I developed, and other non-toy projects. I also added the new blood bag design that I invented while working for AHSA. The blood bag wasn't manufactured, but it showed my ability to invent a new, useful product.

The highlight of my portfolio, however, was the modular children's furniture set I designed and built when I was a sophomore in Ed Zagorski's class. It included the small-scale models of the furniture that I had carefully carved out of four blocks of balsa wood and then painted a glossy red, blue, yellow, or green. I also brought several color slides of kindergarten students playing with the four brightly painted cubes. I owned my own handheld, battery-operated slide viewer so that viewers could clearly see the vibrant images of little children enjoying my colored blocks. I planned to use a small black cloth to conceal the blocks so I could dramatically unveil them after the slide presentation. I was ready.

I had no idea who would conduct my interview, but I went back and reread the *Saturday Evening Post* article about Marvin Glass just in case. It reassured me to believe I had a little understanding of this complicated man. In reality I didn't understand him at all, but I felt in my gut I wanted to work for him. Organized and prepared, I felt confident in both my portfolio and my ability to pitch. I made up my mind that I wasn't walking out of that office without a job.

I knew the salary question would come up if I was lucky enough to be offered a position. I had just been fired from a job paying me $5,500 a year, which was a little more than $100 a week. But I felt destined to be a toy designer. I decided to ask for $10,000 a year, which was a big number in 1967. To strengthen my resolve, I practiced saying the number out loud in front of my mirror. "Ten thousand dollars a year, ten thousand dollars a year," I rehearsed in a normal voice, to make it sound matter-of-fact. I pumped myself up, cheering myself on and repeating, "I'm going to get this job, I'm going to get this job."

A few days before my interview, I checked out Marvin Glass's office space. The building was a two-story limestone fortress with no windows on the ground floor, resembling a giant bank vault. It was located just north of Chicago's business district at 815 N. LaSalle Street, directly across from the Moody Bible Institute.

I arrived early on the big day so I could park and have time to breathe before facing my interviewers. I was scared shitless, but I couldn't let them know that. I was unemployed. I not only wanted this job with Marvin Glass, I needed it.

I rang the doorbell at exactly 10:00 a.m. and got buzzed in immediately. The ground-floor lobby exhibited mirrors, leather sofas, and a fabulous nude female sculpture by Frank Gallo, one of my instructors at the University of Illinois. I was already dazzled and I was just standing in the entrance space. When I climbed the stairs and reached the waiting area, I noticed two Mies van der Rohe leather and stainless-steel Barcelona chairs. I'd studied these in my art history class at Illinois, but this was my first time in front of the real thing. Wow.

Pauline Camberis, the receptionist, had a slender model's figure and long black flowing hair. She wore a full-length dress in a beautiful flowered pattern. She welcomed me warmly and showed me into a conference room through a side door. Pauline said, "Mr. Disko and Mr. Barlow will be right in," turned like a dancer, walked out, and left me alone. She was stunning.

Mr. Disko and Mr. Barlow came in and introduced themselves by their first names, Harry and Gordon, respectively. Harry cut to the chase and said, "Let's see what you have." They were all business as I displayed my portfolio. I knew it was a good sign they let me control the pace and didn't rush me. When you're pitching and the person you're trying to convince starts to turn the sheets of your portfolio for you, you've already lost. My confidence increased when Harry and Gordon didn't hurry me.

My short presentation over, both men commented, "Very nice" and "Good work." Whew! Harry Disko stood and started walking out of the long conference room, saying, "Let me get Mr. Glass." As he left the room, Gordon told me, "Good luck with Marvin." I wasn't sure what he meant, but the way he said "Good luck with Marvin" sent my anxiety level skyrocketing.

I noticed that Harry wore a tie but no jacket, so I took off my suit jacket without loosening my tie. A few minutes later, the door at the end of the room opened and in walked Marvin Glass with a cigarette hanging from his lips. At that time, it was commonplace for people to smoke in the office. Harry Disko, a stocky man with dark, wavy hair, followed.

Marvin wore a beautiful silk tie, custom-made shirt with MG mono-gramed on his cuff, fancy gold and diamond cuff links, and no jacket. He had short brown hair streaked with gray and intelligent brown eyes. He was so skinny his pants were slipping off his hips and he looked unkempt. The *Saturday Evening Post* had lied when they reported that Marvin Glass was five-five. He was more like five-three and weighed about 120 pounds. I was six feet tall and 175 pounds. I towered over Marvin, and when I gave him a firm handshake his small hand was limp. I couldn't believe that *this* diminutive man with a feeble handshake was the titan of the toy inventing business. Could this fifty-two-year-old man really be my dream boss?

"Harry said you have some good work that I should see," Marvin said as he got right to the point. I realized this was the *real* interview. I reminded myself to go slow and not rush. Just as I was about to start, Marvin put up his hand and stopped me. He lifted the phone and asked, "Do you want some coffee?" I replied, "No, thank you," and decided it was a good sign that he wasn't in a hurry. Seconds later, Pauline walked in carrying a sterling silver tray with one cup of coffee and cream and sugar. She must have known he would call for coffee, because she had everything ready. After loading his coffee with lots of cream and four teaspoons of sugar, Marvin stirred, took one sip, set down his cigarette, and said, "OK." I thought, *It's showtime!*

I went through my presentation slowly, making eye contact when I could. He didn't ask a single question. He didn't sip his coffee or pull out another cigarette. My delivery took about five minutes, and when I was done, he looked me in the eye and I looked back. "I would like you to come work for me," Glass said. I was shocked. He paused a moment and asked, "What kind of money are you looking for?" My preparation in front of the mirror kicked in and I answered, "Ten thousand dollars a year." "That's a lot of money for a kid your age," Marvin said. I didn't let my head drop as I replied, "Mister Glass, I'm worth it." With that, he stood up. Glass put his hand out, and when we shook again, his hand was still uncomfortably limp. "OK, you got the job for ten thousand dollars a year. You start next Monday," he said. It was literally that short, and he walked out of the room.

Harry smiled and said, "See you Monday. We start at 7:30 a.m. and don't be late." He led me out the door to Pauline's area. She already knew I was hired and smiled as she said, "See you next Monday." Marvin apparently had told Pauline while I was collecting my things in the conference room.

I believe Marvin hired me instantly because of my presentation of the children's modular furniture. The beautiful four-inch scale model and the Kodachrome slides did the trick. The slides were of a full-scale model being played with by preschool children in a Champaign school room. Marvin's attention shot up when I pitched it. I was sure it was that design that convinced him to hire me.

I walked down the stairs and out of the building, but I could have skipped. I was trying to stay composed until I got on the street and could yell, "YIPPEE!" It wasn't easy, because my heart was racing. When I walked out onto LaSalle Street on Tuesday, April 11, 1967, the sky was clear, the sun was bright, and...then I panicked. I realized I hadn't asked Marvin one single question—*Do I have an office? Can you show me around? How much vacation time do I get? Will I get health insurance?*

None of that mattered. I had just landed my dream job! This was the job I had been thinking about ever since John Spinello told me about the Marvin Glass company when I was a sophomore in Ed Zagorski's design class at the University of Illinois. And I was getting paid a huge $10,000 a year.

It was a morning of pure joy!

Chapter 5

My New Career Is a *Bucket of Fun*

I was on such a high that I practically ran from the interview to share my excitement with Marlene and my family. They were all delighted, but after their cries of "Congratulations!" and "I'm so happy for you!" my folks and Marlene asked me some basic questions. They wondered how much vacation I would get and if I would get health insurance, and I realized I had no idea because I'd forgotten to ask Marvin. My euphoria was such that being told yes was all I had heard.

As their questions continued, I started to sweat. They asked, "What exactly is your job?" and "Do they give you a toy to design?" I realized I didn't know. Then they asked, "Do you have to come up with your own ideas?" and "What do you know about toys in the marketplace?" I panicked when I realized, "Holy shit, I'm a toy designer, now what do I do?"

I realized I had even more questions than my family. I certainly didn't want to call anyone at Marvin Glass for answers. Convincing Marvin that I would be a good toy designer was the easy part. Now I had to figure out what to do! I had a week before my job started, so I had time to conduct research. I had an idea of where to start: Toys "R" Us.

Charles Lazarus was the genius who started Toys "R" Us in 1948 (as Children's Bargaintown; the name was changed in 1957). He was one of the first businessmen to develop big-box specialty stores. His huge success led many others to follow his business model. As these big-box chains came out over the years, I had my own lingo for each store: Home Depot was Hardware "R" Us; Staples was Stationery "R" Us; Best Buy was Electronics "R" Us; Barnes & Noble was Books "R" Us.

I got up the next morning and arrived at Toys "R" Us when their doors opened at 10:00 a.m. It was my first time in the giant toy store. I slowly walked up and down every aisle and then repeated the process. I was overwhelmed as I studied all the categories of toys and games, including preschool, dolls, vehicles, puzzles, crafts, Barbie dolls, and more. I had no children, nieces or nephews, so I had never before bought children's toys.

Even though I had been thinking about being a toy designer for years, it had never occurred to me to spend time in a giant toy store. Toys "R" Us was a lightbulb moment—the toy world on steroids. I knew I was in the right place for a budding toy designer. I spent hours in the aisles before the manager confronted me and asked me what I was doing, because it was clear I wasn't there to buy a toy. I explained I was doing research for my new job as a toy designer with the preeminent toy design company in the world. I showed him toys on the shelves that were Marvin Glass designs, including Rock 'Em Sock 'Em Robots, Light Brite, Mouse Trap, Tip-It, Hands Down, Time Bomb, Kissy Doll, Mr. Machine, Operation, Crazy Clock, Mystery Date, and the Feeley Meeley game.

I showed the manager where each game displayed a little Marvin Glass logo on the side of the box. He thanked me for teaching him something new. He was even more impressed when I told him that one of my classmates had designed the original concept for Operation and sold his idea to Marvin Glass. The manager was kind and told me to spend as much time in the store as I liked. I felt like a cool young kid who had his fifteen minutes of fame at Toys "R" Us. I went to the store every day and after a week I felt more prepared for my first day at work. Later in my career, whenever I needed a toy adrenaline rush, I went to the store. Years later, when I ran MGA and hired new designers, I first sent them to Toys "R" Us. If a designer was in a slump, a trip to the store was the fixer-upper. Ultimately, I bought all the Marvin Glass toys and games I could find and studied them at home.

During the week I spent wandering around Toys "R" Us, I learned that many names of toys and games were sayings, expressions, or idioms. The guy that beat me at ping-pong back in college beat me "hands down." Hands Down was also the name of a Marvin Glass game staring at me from the shelf. The game with that name contained four little plastic paddles in the shape of small hands that you slapped down. The slowest hand down lost a card to another player. The game had more rules than that, but that was the essence, the magic. It was a big hit for MGA and the Ideal Toy Company back in the early '60s.

Ed Zagorski had taught me how to come up with solutions by teaching me how to ask the right questions to get there. I thought about him as I looked at the titles and puzzled out how they had developed these games and toys. I wondered if the designer at Glass first thought of the idiom or the mechanism of the game? I kept thinking about it and had an idea for a game called What Came First, The Chicken or the Egg? It consisted of a little box filled with small plastic chickens and tiny white marbles, which were the eggs. The box had a hole in the bottom, and when you shook the box, the players would bet on what would come out first. It was a lousy idea, but the process worked.

What I learned before I started at Glass was that I needed a process to create a toy or game. I wrote down a list of idioms to use as a source of inspiration without knowing where that list might lead me. My list included:

At the drop of a hat
Pulling my leg
Ball in your court
Barking up the wrong tree

Cry over spilled milk
Miss the boat
Hit the nail on the head
Cross that bridge when you come to it
Beat around the bush
Curiosity killed the cat
Let sleeping dogs lie

and

Ants in the pants

I showed up at MGA on Monday, April 17, 1967, at 7:30 a.m. I didn't wear a tie or a jacket. I brought my head, two hands, and an ultra-competitive desire to succeed. Harry Disko was waiting for me when I buzzed the front door. Pauline, the receptionist, wasn't in yet and I also assumed Marvin didn't arrive early. It was a much earlier start time than I was used to at American Hospital Supply Corporation, but my jump in salary more than made up for the inconvenience.

Harry led me into the conference room and explained the company's simple hierarchy. Marvin was the unquestioned heart and soul of the company and stood alone at the top of the pyramid. Then came his five partners. I was in the third tier, the toy designers, who were, to my delight, paid to dream up fun stuff. Next came the model makers who built the toys, and who I quickly learned were essential to my hopes of achieving an outstanding career. Along with the receptionists and bookkeepers, we had about seventy employees total.

All of the employees were men, other than Pauline and the bookkeeper. I thought it was strange that we didn't employ any female toy designers, because half of our customers were little girls. Women executives and designers were still rare in the business world in the late 1960s, but I thought we would benefit from hiring women. I never dreamed then that one day I would be in a position to change our company hiring practices.

Harry placed a six-page document in front of me and told me to sign it. In essence, it said two things: that every idea I had belonged to Marvin Glass, and that our company functioned with the secrecy of a Swiss bank. If I had a toy or game idea outside of the office, it belonged to Glass. If I had an idea in my dreams, in the shower, or on vacation, it belonged to Glass. Marvin Glass owned my imagination—lock, stock, and barrel.

If I talked to anyone outside of work about anything I was working on, including my wife, family, or friends, I would be fired immediately. If I lost my keys, I would be fired. If I forgot to lock up, I would be fired. Whatever I was working on during the day had to be locked up at night in the fortified walk-in vault. I couldn't believe it—they had a vault for toys!

I signed the form and our tour began. Harry led me through the conference room and into the inner sanctum of toy design and manufacturing—the machine shop. When I walked through the door I was amazed. The shop was gigantic, much bigger than I'd ever imagined, and the space was filled with vibrant primary colors. In the center of the vast room stood industrial-sized drill presses, band saws, milling machines, and lathes. Each machine was brightly painted in red, blue, yellow, or green. I heard the familiar metallic sounds—the grinding, growling, and screeching of heavy machinery in use. Ringed around the outside walls of the cavernous room were the cluttered and cheerfully painted workbenches of the model makers. In some places, model makers and toy designers huddled together working on their projects. The shop looked like Santa's North Pole workshop but was filled with men in jeans and gray shop coats instead of elves in green hats!

We had model makers instead of elves, but they did the same thing as Santa's helpers—bring our ideas to life. There were about twenty model makers who, between them, used five lathes, four milling machines, three disc sanders, three drill presses, and two band saws. Each machine was known by its color, so there was "the green drill press," "the blue drill press," and "the red drill press." Unlike in Leonard's gray machine shop at the University of Illinois, no one here had to wait to use the equipment. It was a delightful and cheerful place to design and build toy prototypes.

Everyone shook hands and warmly welcomed me into their private and secret world. The only employees allowed to see inside the toy design studio were those who worked inside it. Even Pauline, who had worked for Marvin for years and was his secretary and dear friend, was never allowed in the design studio.

I knew I wasn't going to remember the names of all the model makers after meeting them once, so I didn't worry about it. But I learned and remembered the name of the shop foreman on the first day—Gus Demeyer. Gus lectured me sternly, "If you don't know your ass about using a machine, come and ask me and don't fuck up the equipment. Don't cut off any fingers and get blood in my shop." I nodded and said, "OK. Thanks, Gus." Gus replied, "Your ass." It turned out to be his favorite expression. He had a limited vocabulary. Gus was *bah humbug* about everything, but I grew to like and respect his knowledge of machinery and equipment. I certainly wasn't going to mix paint on any of his drill presses. That would be "my ass!"

The next man I remembered was a tall, handsome man with a firm grip and wide smile, Flynn Barr. He was introduced as the chauffeur, the maintenance man, Marvin's man, and the head of public relations for the studio. I liked him immediately and we became great friends.

Harry then led me upstairs to his office on the second floor, where the partners' offices were located. He showed me his little black book, which was full of job numbers, not phone numbers. He explained that every toy or game project was assigned a number and entered into his book. Harry opened it up and showed me the first job number assigned in 1967 was 67-001. The 67 for was for the year and 001 was for the first project. He said that the Glass studio typically generated around 700 numbers a year. I was impressed and said, "Wow! That's a lot of projects." Next to the number was the name of the designer, followed by a brief description. It was easy to rewrite the description if the project changed as we worked on it. Harry told me to see him for a job number if I had an idea.

Harry handed me a bound 1967 calendar with my name on the front cover and told me to use it to keep track of my hours on each job number. Time was broken down into thirty-minute increments. MGA paid every two weeks, and the bookkeeper announced that calendars had to be turned in on Wednesday if you wanted to be paid on Friday. If you didn't turn in your calendar, you didn't get paid.

As Harry talked, I learned that he had served in the Air Force in World War II and was known around the office as the "Sarge." He had started at MGA years before as a model maker and worked his way up to be a partner and Marvin's right-hand man. Harry and his little black book ran the back of the studio with a tough but talented hand.

Harry next showed me to my office and told me that I'd be sharing space with David, a big guy from New York. Harry said I'd start by helping David with one of his current projects. David's project turned out to be uninspiring—an aluminum mold that made little clay bricks, which you then baked in an oven warmed with a light bulb. When the little clay bricks hardened, you'd build things with them, similar to an Easy-Bake Oven. It was actually worse than it sounded. I thought that it must not be too difficult to get a job number if David's idea could get one.

David explained that I could log some time every week to miscellaneous projects that weren't assigned a number, but I shouldn't waste too much time on them. I realized that if I came up with my own idea and got a job number from Harry, then I could work on my own project. Without new ideas, I'd end up working on someone else's project, like making little clay bricks. I decided to get my first job number the next day.

I told David I wanted to get the lay of the land and he suggested I see Gus, who ran the machine shop. Gus directed me to a corner filled with hundreds of disassembled toys, dolls, and games. When I looked around, I could hardly believe it—I was in toy junkyard heaven! There was a bin of toy truck wheels of all sizes and shapes, and another of Hot Wheels and Matchbox cars. There was one bin filled with doll heads, another with doll limbs, and another overflowing with doll bodies. Searching through the toy bins was like hitting the jackpot on the nickel slot machine that my dad brought home for me. I felt like I was eight years old again, but now I was getting paid to play with toys. Pinch me!

I could help myself to anything, but it was a large plastic beach bucket that caught my eye. Suddenly, an idea just popped into my head.

I imagined little kids laughing as they scurried around a room picking up different-colored balls that had been flung out of the bucket. I pictured the kids running back and forth and dropping their balls back into the bucket one at a time. The first child to get all their balls in the bucket wins.

What if I figured out how to make a plastic bucket that could mechanically toss differently colored balls around a room? Each kid would be assigned a different colored ball, and they would run back and forth to place their balls back in the pail one at a time. There would be four colors and four balls of each color. The first kid to get their four balls in the pail wins. I thought about calling the game Drop in the Bucket. Nah, that was a lousy name. "Drop in the bucket" is an idiom meaning an insufficient amount in comparison to what is needed. I knew I needed a better name, but first I'd build a prototype out of stuff I found in the toy junkyard.

I found sixteen colored balls that were the size of ping-pong balls, four each of red, blue, yellow, and green. I tossed them in a plastic bucket, found a wind-up mechanism with a coiled spring to use as the mechanical basis for the tossing apparatus, and headed up to my office to build a mock-up of my idea.

The next morning, I went in search of Harry to get a job number. If your idea didn't have a name, you could just describe it briefly. I didn't want to use Drop in the Bucket, so I intended to tell Harry I needed a job number for "Bucket that throws colored balls that kids pick up and bring back to the bucket." Happily, inspiration struck me the moment I walked into Harry's office. Ideas come at the strangest times! Out of the blue, I told Harry I needed a job number for my first project, titled Bucket of Fun. I told him to make sure to put my name, Jeffrey, after the number. That was my first job number. I never again worked on David's clay-brick oven. From that day forward, I only worked on my own projects.

In the world of toy and game design there are two parts to a successful product: the raw concept and the execution. Sometimes there's a concept so great and pure that anyone can profitably execute the idea. Sometimes there's an OK idea with fantastic execution that succeeds beyond anyone's imagination. Most great toys and games, however, are born of a terrific concept and fabulous execution. Here are some examples:

Let's say I had a brilliant concept for a toy made of a hollow circle of lightweight plastic tubing, about as big around as an adult bicycle tire. The user picks up the plastic tube, puts it around their waist, sets it spinning, and gyrates their hips to try to keep it from falling to the ground. Wham-O, a terrific company, introduced the Hula Hoop in 1957. They priced it perfectly at $1.98 and sold more than 100 million hoops in the first two years. Wham-O has now sold billions of hoops. The Hula Hoop is a great and pure concept, but the execution was simple and anyone could have made it. Sadly, it wasn't MGA.

How about a toy with an OK concept and fabulous execution? Imagine two plastic robot boxers moving about in a ring, punching each other until one wins the fight. The idea by itself isn't worth a lot. Then MGA partner Burt Meyer and some model makers got hold of the concept and turned it into gold. They first figured out how to control each robot mechanically. That meant each player could move their own robot around the boxing ring and make it punch when they wanted it to. But instead of making the other robot fall down when it was punched, it was easier and funnier to make the robot's head pop up off its shoulders while making a funny buzzing noise. The boxers, one blazing red and the other turquoise, fought in a bright yellow ring surrounded by ropes. This concept became Rock 'Em Sock 'Em Robots, and it was a blockbuster toy in the early '60s for the Louis Marx toy company. Happily for us, MGA designed the robot game, and it still sells today.

One last example. A plastic bucket is filled with four each of four different-colored plastic balls, red, blue, yellow, and green. Each child picks a color. Children gather in a circle around the bucket and one child turns a knob. After a ten-second delay, which gives everyone time to get in place, the knob releases a latch and the bucket flings the balls all around the room. The kids chase after their colored balls and bring them back to the bucket. The first one to retrieve all of their balls wins. Sound familiar?

For me, creating the concept for Bucket of Fun was the easy part. Now came the hard part—the execution of my idea. The real challenge to Bucket of Fun was in figuring out how to make the pail toss the balls around the room after a slight delay. When the child turned the knob, there needed to be a delay of a few seconds before the device activated and the balls flew out of the bucket. That way, all the kids had time to get in position around the bucket before the balls went flying. I thought a ten-second delay would be perfect. I mocked up the idea with the plastic beach pail I'd picked up in the toy junkyard.

I first cemented a plastic post in the center of the bucket's floor. I decided to use one of the Chinese wind-up coil spring mechanisms I had found in Gus's office for the timing device, or escapement. I then spent a week trying to design a latch that would shoot the plastic balls out of the bucket after a ten-second delay, but despite trying everything I could think of, I couldn't get it right.

I told Harry that I needed a model maker to help me figure out how to design the right latch. Harry gave me Eugene Jaworski, a dark-haired Russian immigrant who was a few years older than I. Eugene grew up in Brazil and spoke Russian, Portuguese, and reasonably good English with a Russian accent. He was about five-seven and slender, with a sunny, laughing disposition. His father, Nikolai, was also a model maker at MGA. I loved working with Eugene and soon realized how lucky I was to have him on my team.

First, Eugene and I had to figure out how to build a latch that would release remotely. Eugene tinkered with the idea until he invented a fabulous latch mechanism that solved our tricky problem. It securely held the balls in place in the bucket until the player triggered the latch remotely. Then the latch would suddenly release, and the balls would shoot up into the air.

Our next step was to invent the mechanism that would cause the latch to release on command. I drilled a small hole in the side of the bucket near the bottom, under the plastic disc that the balls sat on top of inside the bucket. We then ran a thin string from the latch through the hole to outside of the pail, five feet away. To test it, I put the balls on the plastic disc and yanked the string. The disc shot up and the balls flew out. We were getting close, but the string idea was just to test the remote release. We had to get rid of the string.

Eugene and I replaced the string with a thin plastic bar that ran parallel to the floor. We built the device so that when the child looked at the bucket, they would see a colorful knob on the side of the pail. The child would turn the knob and that would cause the wind-up spring mechanism to start ticking. Ten seconds later…*blammo!* The spring mechanism released the latch holding the disc in place, the disc flew up and stopped abruptly, and the sixteen balls flew out of the bucket.

We had one remaining problem to solve. When the knob was turned and the disc was released, most of the balls shot straight up into the air but many fell back down into the bucket. I needed the balls to scatter all over the room. The solution Eugene and I devised was to change the shape of the plastic stopper at the top of the post. Instead of the flat piece of plastic we had been using, we added an angled piece to the stopper. It was shaped like an upside-down V. That way, when the balls flew up into the air, they would bounce off the angled piece of plastic and fly out in all directions into the room. My first toy was born—Bucket of Fun!

As we worked, I noticed that other designers kept stopping by Eugene's bench. They wanted to know when he would be done working with me, because they wanted to collaborate with him on their projects. Eugene was a remarkably talented model maker who always did more than was asked of him. He came up with creative solutions to problems and always made his projects better. Even though he had the ability to be a toy designer, as a model maker he didn't face the unrelenting pressure that we did. The heart of the company was the constant need to develop new, profitable toy ideas, and he didn't want to deal with the stress, so, to my good fortune, Eugene remained a model maker.

I didn't want to lose Eugene to another toy designer, so I spent my days working by his bench on the first floor. The machine shop was where the action was. It was here that the model makers plied their trade among the candy-colored but powerful drill presses, lathes, and saws. Their workbenches overflowed with hand tools, gadgets, and bits and pieces of toys. They banged and sawed and screwed and puttered, trying to manipulate a gizmo or a piece of plastic to do this or that. The shop floor was a busy hive of construction, a place where every dream seemed like a real possibility.

Marvin was watching our progress on Bucket of Fun and must have liked what he saw, because he told Harry Disko to assign a second model maker to speed up the completion of my project. I soon discovered why: the senior VP of development for the Milton Bradley Company, Mel Taft, was due in the office in a few weeks. Marvin wanted Bucket of Fun ready in time to show it to Mel Taft. Wow! My first toy would be shown to Milton Bradley! I was even more thrilled when I learned that I would personally present Bucket of Fun to Mel Taft, who would soon be arriving at our studio on LaSalle Street.

MGA was unusual because our clients traveled to Chicago from all over the world to see our toy inventions. We never went to them to pitch our ideas. Our clients loved being pampered by Marvin, who treated them like royalty. When the day of my first presentation arrived, Flynn Barr, our chauffeur, picked up Mel Taft from Chicago's O'Hare airport. By the time Mel got to the studio he was in a great mood. Flynn was beyond charming and had a great infectious laugh. Everyone enjoyed Flynn's company, and we considered him our ambassador. Occasionally, clients would warn Marvin, "If Flynn isn't the one picking me up at the airport, I'm not coming in." They weren't kidding.

I had less than a month on the job and I was thrilled that I was getting the chance to personally pitch my toy invention to Mr. Taft. One of Marvin's brilliant ideas was to have the designer who developed the project carry it into the conference room, then pitch it to the client himself. If the client loved it, you knew it—you heard his praise and experienced the thrill of clinching a sale. If the client didn't like it, you heard the flatness of his rejection and knew you had to get back to work. I had a good feeling about Bucket of Fun, and I was nervous but ready when I walked into the conference room to meet with Mel Taft and Marvin.

I spent a few minutes showing Bucket of Fun to Mel, but then it was time for action. We handed the prototype to Mel and brought in a few other employees to play the game with us. Mel turned the knob and within seconds we were all running around the room laughing and chasing colored plastic balls. We were playing like six-year-olds! Being a child again was not a bad way to make a living back in 1967.

Mel loved it and wanted Bucket of Fun shipped to Milton Bradley in Springfield, Massachusetts. He was confident Milton Bradley would produce the game and have it ready in time for the next international toy fair, in February in New York. Mel was right. I was at the next Toy Fair New York and saw Bucket of Fun displayed by Milton Bradley for the whole world to see. In Milton Bradley's final design, the bucket was bright orange and the balls were colored bright red, soft yellow, sea green, and sky blue. The box was white with Bucket of Fun spelled out in different-colored letters and a drawing of colored balls flying out of a bucket. The original box shouted, "EXCITING ACTION—INDOORS OR OUT! Magic bucket pops out a shower of balls—players scramble to retrieve them!!" My first toy design was also my first sale. When would I sell my next invention? I was hooked for life!

Chapter 6

Game Design

The Difference Between Skill and Luck

Within a few weeks I discovered that almost everything we designed was work to be shown to the next client who was coming in for a presentation. If your model maker was working on a project that wasn't ready to be shown within a few days, you often lost your model maker temporarily to a more advanced project. The date and timing of client presentations determined the flow of work at the studio. We would usually have one client presentation a week, perhaps two, but no more than that, because the studio couldn't keep up a faster pace. We rarely went more than two or three weeks without any client presentations at all. Everything we did was to create toys and games to show our next clients. Remarkably, we kept up the unrelenting pace year after year.

I loved the rush of presenting my own inventions to clients. I thrived on the excitement of presenting an exciting idea to enthusiastic buyers. Marvin understood that all of his creative designers loved to hear their work praised, and he generously shared both money and compliments with us. We all loved him for it. He knew how to motivate his employees—that was the essential ingredient to the success of MGA.

Our most valuable commodity was time. The only product we sold was new ideas for toys and games. Marvin gave his inventors time and motivation to dream up great new products, and we often did. Our clients included major toy and game manufacturers such as Milton Bradley, Parker Brothers, Ideal Toy, Fisher-Price, Mattel, Playskool, and more. They kept returning to our Chicago office, buying our products, and paying us royalties for one reason: we repeatedly churned out great ideas that made money, sometimes a lot of it.

The toy design business operates a lot like the movie business—we're "creatives," in entertainment industry jargon. Just five or six profitable hits a year pay for the entire studio, and behind every hit are hundreds of ideas that don't make it. Every year we generated 700 or 800 ideas in the job book. Of those, we built and presented 100 to 150 prototypes to clients—sometimes we'd show the same prototype to six or seven clients before deciding that the idea wouldn't work. We signed thirty to thirty-five licensing agreements each year with toy manufacturers.

Then the manufacturers set to work. They perfected our idea and manufactured a final product in time to show it at Toy Fair New York, held annually in February. Tens of thousands of toy ideas were presented to major retailers every year, and toys lived or died based on what the retailers decided. The five or six major retailers, including Toys "R" Us, Walmart, Kmart, Sears, and KB Toys, sent the toy into either living rooms or oblivion. The last hurdle was selling the parents. Was this the right toy to buy for their boy or girl? It was our job to convince them to say yes.

Harry Disko was the keeper of "the list," the all-important list of projects that were to be shown to the next client coming in. The list was fluid, a work in progress always subject to change at the last moment. Rough mock-ups were often shown to clients. Sometimes, when the client meeting was not going well, Harry would come out of the conference room with a look of desperation on his face. He had to try to save the meeting with a surprise winner. He'd come to us frantically seeking anything that could be shown to the client and turn the meeting into a success. Sometimes it was a project that Marvin never even saw until it was carried into the room, but Marvin was great at jumping right in like he had known about the project all along. Over time, I built up a backlog of mock-up ideas that Harry could use if he walked out of the conference room with "the look."

I was determined to always have a project ready to show and pitch at the next client conference. Maybe the idea wasn't great or wasn't executed well, but at least it was on Harry's job list, and that was important to Marvin. If several weeks passed and you weren't in the conference room pitching as clients came and went, you could bet your ass you either needed to get busy or you'd be gone. The only way our company survived was by producing a lot of ideas.

I quickly understood the underlying process of designing games for Marvin Glass and soon made my own list of guiding principles, including:

- Work on your own ideas.
- Work on projects for the next client presentation.
- Teamwork: when co-designers are stuck, help them. Then they'll help you when you're stuck.
- Work on multiple ideas at once—the more, the better.
- Don't fall too much in love with your ideas, because most fail.
- Don't log too much time on any one project. If it's not working, stop.
- The job comes before anything else. Make Marvin happy. Marvin's only life is toys, so don't talk about sports, television, or movies in the studio.
- Be a team player, because if the company does well, so will you.
- Forty-hour workweeks are a myth. Plan on working sixty or seventy hours per week. If you wear a watch, don't let Marvin see you looking at it. Don't ask for time off.

I also quickly came to believe one basic fact: we needed to hire women to be toy designers. I couldn't get past the idea that half of our customers were little girls. I thought this was a major weakness in our company that could be easily remedied. I also knew enough to keep my opinion to myself for the time being, but I asked Ed Zagorski to keep his eyes open for talented women designers in his class at the University of Illinois.

I soon became known as a prolific idea man. Eugene and I were adept at transforming my designs into viable prototypes that often sold to manufacturers. I had worked at Marvin Glass for four months by the time August arrived and summer was ending. We were getting ready to send a contract to Milton Bradley for my first project, Bucket of Fun, and I had created other games that were almost ready for presentation. Among them were Dynamite Shack, Penguin Polo, Big Mouth, Who You? and Humor Rumor.

A great game is one you can open and start playing immediately. No one likes reading game rules. I kept this in mind and discovered that it was easy for me to generate game concepts and build prototypes. The toy and game industry now depended heavily on television advertising to sell our products, and I knew that our inventions had to be three-dimensional and vibrant. I had grown up playing with Tinkertoys and Erector Sets, and their design principles were embedded in my brain. My ideas kept flowing and Eugene and I became a productive, thriving team. I pulled lots of new job numbers and things couldn't be better for me at work.

My expertise was designing games more than toys. Games are more interesting to me because they're often more social than toys, which are sometimes individualistic. When playing games, players learn to win and lose and cooperate with other people. I had a knack for designing preschool games in particular. It was easy for me to think of fun games for little kids to play. The trick was to structure the game so that each player thought he or she had a chance to win.

There is a difference between skill and luck. The only complex game of pure skill is chess. Checkers is a game of skill, but the pieces are all the same. Tic-tac-toe is skill, but there is no way for good players to win. For every other game, the designer wants to make each player believe, "If I win it's because I'm skilled" and "If I lose it's because they were lucky." It was my job to find the right balance between skill and luck in every game I designed.

My career was blossoming and I had a wonderful routine at work. I was making toys and being introduced to industry giants at the same time. These giants included Lionel Weintraub, the president of Ideal Toy Company. Lionel was the son-in-law of the founders, Morris and Rose Michtom. The company started in Queens and introduced the teddy bear to America in 1903, in honor of President Theodore Roosevelt. Ideal has been a robust family business ever since.

Lionel Weintraub made it possible for Marvin Glass to become a wealthy man. The two men were great friends in the 1940s, and Lionel was Marvin's first important client. Lionel launched Marvin's career as an independent toy designer. They enjoyed a mutually profitable relationship and both Ideal and MGA flourished. Lionel was a sophisticated, beautifully dressed, friendly man with gray hair. Unlike some of our clients, however, who loved to play every game we pitched to them, Lionel would never dream of getting down on the floor to play with the toys we showed him.

I thrived as a toy designer because I intuitively understood the *process* of designing toys. I knew that the most difficult thing to accept in any creative business was the harsh reality that most ideas fail. In most other professions, failure is unacceptable. But creative people hear the word "no" a lot more often than they hear "yes." I was never deterred by a "no." In the toy design business, I could fail, brush myself off, and try again. It's acceptable to fail 90 percent of the time as long as you capitalize on the 10 percent of your ideas that are winners.

Things couldn't have been going any better, but I had one constant worry. I could be drafted any day. My draft deferment had expired in April 1967. In August, after a few months of great fun and growth at MGA, reality hit me between the eyes when I received a letter from the Selective Service Office. It took me a day or two before I could bring myself to open the envelope. It was what I feared—the dreadful notification from the draft board that I could be drafted at any time.

I was devastated. If I didn't think of something, my new life and brilliant career could be over almost before it started. I saw only one possibility that might preclude me from being drafted and still allow me to continue working for Marvin at night—I would teach in a Chicago public school. I didn't tell Marvin my idea until the last moment.

Chicago faced a critical shortage of teachers in the fall of 1967. The Chicago Board of Education was so desperate, they developed an emergency program called "Provisional Teachers." If you had a college degree in any subject, you were eligible to teach elementary school for the Chicago Public Schools. The only requirements were that you had to pass a physical exam and agree to take education classes. Crucially, teachers under this program were given a draft deferment.

Before I knew it, I was at the Chicago Board of Education building and in front of an elderly woman who was about to administer my physical exam. She took my blood pressure and pulse and said, "All that's left are the vision and hearing tests." There was no optical equipment, just the standard eye chart on the wall. I stood in front of the chart and she said, "Take five steps back and read the letters." I read a few rows and passed.

The last test was hearing. This is precisely what happened—I couldn't possibly make this up. But Chicago was beyond desperate for school-teachers in 1967. They had to have adults standing in the classrooms when the students returned from summer vacation in a month. The woman asked me to go to the opposite side of the small room and look out the window facing away from her. I had no idea what was happening. She then whispered softly, "Can you hear me?" I almost exploded with laughter and barely controlled myself before I whispered, "Yes, I can hear you." That was the end of my hearing test. I think the only real requirement for passing the physical was breathing. I got my provisional certificate and was assigned to teach fourth grade at William Cullen Bryant Elementary School at 1355 South Kedvale Avenue, a poor black neighborhood on the West Side of Chicago.

Now I had two jobs and needed to break the news to Marvin. My plan was to teach during the day, then work after school at the toy studio on Monday, Wednesday, and Friday, and all day on Saturday. On Tuesdays and Thursdays, I had to attend education classes at the Board of Education from 8:00 until 10:00 p.m. With Sunday off, I would spend almost forty hours a week designing toys. I hoped my plan would work.

I steadied myself and walked in to tell Marvin. I was relieved when he took the news well, expressing concern for my safety and survival. He opposed the Vietnam War. I told him I could continue to be productive if I could keep working with my model maker, Eugene. Marvin agreed, then encouraged me to get serious about having kids. He reminded me that if Marlene got pregnant, I'd qualify for a prospective-father deferment and could stop teaching. Marvin smiled when he said, "You would be creating another consumer for our toys." He added, "If Marlene calls and she's ovulating, Flynn will drive you home immediately." That's when I broke into a smile. I needed all the humor I could get, because my fourth-grade class was going to descend upon me in thirty days.

I wanted to get the kids on my side on the first day of school, so I headed to my old standby, Toys "R" Us, to look for ideas. I was in the puzzle section when I spied a Milton Bradley Superman cardboard picture puzzle. It was one hundred pieces, the perfect size for fourth-graders. I bought four boxes of identical Superman puzzles, and now I had a plan for the first day of school.

I started teaching on the Tuesday after Labor Day in 1967. I arrived at Bryant Elementary School early to check out my classroom. It was on the third floor, because the older kids had classrooms on the upper floors. I found my room and wasn't surprised to find it was in bad shape. It had chalkboards on three sides and windows on the fourth wall. I had one small desk and there were a lot of desk/chair combos for the students.

I still have my own eighth-grade graduation class picture from Hibbard Elementary School in Albany Park. There were ninety-six white kids in my class. I think it was the same at Niles Township High School. That morning, when the bell rang and my classroom door opened, thirty-six black nine-year-old children poured into the room. All the students in the school were black. The only white, Asian, or Latino people in the school were teachers. That's the way it was in Chicago in 1967.

I welcomed the students, introduced myself, and described my after-school job as a toy designer. I told them I started teaching to help me generate ideas for toy designs, although I knew these children were too poor to receive any toys designed by Marvin Glass & Associates. I didn't tell the kids the real reason I was teaching—to avoid the draft.

I asked the students to stand and split into four groups. I took a deck of playing cards and pulled out nine cards of each suit, shuffled, and had each kid pick a card. The four teams were made up of the clubs, diamonds, spades, and hearts. They loved the fairness of this. Random decision maker strikes again!

Each group put four desks together to create a larger surface area to work on. I placed identical one-hundred-piece puzzles of Superman on each of the surfaces and explained, "Before I give you the go-ahead, this puzzle exercise is a lesson in cooperation. If you cooperate with your teammates in putting the puzzle together, you'll complete it before the other teams and get a prize. Cooperation means if someone is working on the border pieces and you find an outside piece, you give your piece to that person. If you're working on Superman's face, other players will give you face pieces. Without cooperation, your team will come in last place. The puzzles are identical. If you're missing a piece, it probably fell on the floor. Remember—cooperation. GO!" The students loved the puzzle game and I often used it as a reward for good class behavior. I frequently employed games to teach cooperation.

We worked on reading, math, and science. Most of the students were reading at a second- or third-grade level. No one was reading fourth-grade material. I brought a small record player to the classroom so we could study music and also provided materials for art projects.

One day, when I'd only been teaching a few weeks, I was assigned to watch the kids on the playground during recess. I noticed two little kids punching each other hard. I broke up the fight and one of the kids looked up at me and said, "Get your mother-fucking white hands off of me." I was shocked. I had heard those words before, but never from a

· six-year-old. All I could say was, "OK," and walked away. I went to the principal, explained what had happened, and said that I would never again go out for recess duty. She agreed, but told me I should have let the kids just fight it out.

After a few months, I prepared for parents night. I decorated the classroom and readied my files on each of my thirty-six students. That night only one parent, a mother, showed up. I was devastated. I also quickly realized that my night education classes were useless. They taught me nothing about how to help my students learn, and I stopped attending them.

As a teacher, the hardest thing for me to accept was that most of the kids weren't going to learn anything from me. Teaching in the classroom wasn't hard, but it was very difficult when I couldn't reach the students. I wanted to help them but I couldn't. On the other hand, designing toys was easy. It was 180 degrees from teaching. The contrast between the miserable working conditions in a Chicago public school and the coziness of the Marvin Glass studios was brutal.

The school faculty was about half black and half white, and I got to know one of the black teachers in the classroom next to me. Anthony Brown also worked an after-school job, and it happened to be at the downtown post office, which was right on the way to my LaSalle Street office. We became friends when I drove Anthony to the post office so he didn't have to take the bus.

On April 4, 1968, James Earl Ray assassinated Martin Luther King Jr. as King stood on the balcony of a motel in Memphis. King died around 7:00 p.m. He was only thirty-nine years old. I didn't hear the news that night and I went to school the next day unaware of King's death. That morning, older kids ran down the school halls screaming that King had been shot and killed. The principal came over the school public address system and told the teachers to send our kids home immediately. She said she was closing the school and that the teachers should leave. As usual, I looked for my friend Anthony Brown to give him a ride to the post office.

The streets were already filling up with upset and angry people. Anthony and I tried to avoid the crowds by slowly driving north down a small street, but older kids threw stones at us and jumped on the car. Anthony and I were scared to death, and I was glad my friend was with me and I wasn't alone. We saw kids starting fires in empty buildings and realized the entire neighborhood was beginning to be set ablaze. We got out of there just in time.

The fires on the West Side of Chicago worsened as the day progressed. Chicago, Detroit, Baltimore, and Washington, D.C., experienced major riots. In Chicago, eleven people died. Nationwide, thirty-nine people were killed. The school didn't reopen until several days later, after the riots had died down and the fires were extinguished. I was relieved and glad when the school year ended.

Shortly after King was murdered, Robert F. Kennedy was shot by an assassin in Los Angeles on June 5, 1968, and died the next day. The summer became filled with protests and upheavals around the country, including during the Democratic National Convention, which Chicago hosted from August 26 to 29. Violent riots broke out along the lakefront, with the Chicago police confronting 10,000 active demonstrators. The unrest lasted for days. 1968 was an awful year for the nation, for Chicago, and for me.

The outside world was a mess, but the design studio served as my escape. I worked there every free minute during the school year and pumped out a lot of designs. But when I returned to the Chicago Board of Education in the summer of 1968 to get my job back at Bryant School, they refused to rehire me because I had quit night school. The Board of Ed didn't care that I thought the teaching classes were a waste of time.

I panicked, thinking I would soon be drafted, but Marlene got me a job teaching shop class at her junior high school in suburban Elk Grove Village. I gave my students some projects from Zagorski's design curriculum and they loved them. So did I. It was quite a change from my inner-city experience. Soon enough, Marlene was pregnant, and in October 1968 I got an expectant-father draft deferment. I left teaching and returned to Marvin Glass and the toy business, where I would happily remain for the next forty years. I couldn't foresee, however, that on the day I returned to Glass full time, my single greatest toy design was on the horizon.

Chapter 7

Inventing *Ants in the Pants*

■ ▬ ▬ ▬ ▬ ▬ ▬ ▬ ▬ ▬ ■

I needed fresh ideas when I returned to Marvin Glass full time in the fall of 1968. My job was to come up with a design to sell a piece of plastic. My hope was to invent a "perennial," which is a product that is sold on the market for at least three years. I succeeded beyond my wildest dreams.

I pulled out my list of idioms for inspiration and the phrase "Ants in the Pants" kept running through my mind. I kept repeating the words and an idea suddenly popped into my head for a game for preschoolers. What if each player has a certain number of plastic ants, each with their own color? I would design a pair of hollow pants about the height of a Quaker Oats container. The pants would stand up on their legs and players would try to send their ants flying up into the pants. The first player to get all of their ants into the pants wins. Figuring out how the players would try to flip their ants up into the pants would be my main challenge. I loved this idea!

One of the first things I learned as a toy designer is that the biggest issue in designing profitable toys is cost. Toy designs had to be inexpensive if we were to have any chance of selling them to a client. The greatest tension, delay, and expense in toy designing is simplifying the production process and reducing the manufacturing cost. The hard-costs-to-retail-sales-price ratio was about one to five ("hard costs" were how much money the toy manufacturer had to spend on materials and manufacturing to put the toy in the box, ready to sell). We always worked backwards from the anticipated retail sales price. In 1968, $9.95 was considered a lot to pay for a game, and I thought a good price point for Ants in the Pants was $7.50. I worked to bring Ants in the Pants in at $1.50 in hard costs.

I used the same design principle for Ants in the Pants that I had for Bucket of Fun. I decided to create a total of sixteen ants, four each of four different colors—red, yellow, blue, and green, just as I had used sixteen balls of four different colors for Bucket of Fun. I started sketching ants in different shapes, and settled on a simple design that showed an ant from above, consisting of a head, body, and six legs. The ant design didn't need to be realistic—preschoolers have vivid imaginations.

Once I was happy with my sketch of my prototype ant, I cut out the design from the piece of paper and attached it to a thin piece of plastic by using two-sided sticky masking tape. Our machine shop was stocked with plastic sheets that came in all sizes and thicknesses, and with our jigsaws, milling machines, and belt sanders, we could cut the plastic into any shape. Then we could machine, vacuum form, and cement the plastic shapes to build our models. I used a jigsaw to cut out my first ant, which was about two inches long and had six legs. Now I had to figure out how to make the ant jump up into the pants.

My first thought was to use a teeter-totter. I built a simple device and put an ant on one side of the teeter-totter, then tapped the other side with my finger. It flipped my ant up into the air, but it usually flew straight up or backwards, not forward where the hollow pants were standing. No good.

I next designed a miniature catapult, similar in design to what the class had built in Zagorski's sophomore design class to launch our "space capsule." It worked, but it required two hands, took too long, and was too expensive. I needed a better idea to flip the ants into the pants.

I turned to the game of tiddlywinks for inspiration. In the shop, we had an unusual tool that used heat to bend plastic. It was made from a two-foot-long, thin piece of rigid wire, which would become very hot when it was heated by plugging it into an electrical socket. When a model maker laid a piece of plastic on top of the hot wire, the plastic became soft and flexible where the heat was applied and could be folded along any angle.

I drew a line down the center of my plastic ant, from head to tail. I applied the heated wire to the center line and bent my ant into an inverted V shape. When I reached the angle I liked, about sixty degrees, I held the ant under water to cool it. The thin plastic retained its new shape and I set it on the workbench. My ant was now standing on its six thin legs. The plastic body bent easily when I pushed it down with my finger, and when I released my finger, it jumped up in the air all by itself. My ant was now a one-piece, jumping "tiddlywink." Essentially, my game was tiddlywinks, but much, much cuter.

My last task was to figure out how to make the ant jump forward instead of straight up into the air. I worked on it and realized that if I shortened the front legs by a fraction, the ant would jump forward. Eugene and I had continued our blossoming partnership, and I brought him in to make the sixteen plastic ants so I could turn my attention to designing the pants.

I thought the pants should be about the height of a Quaker Oats container, which is just over nine inches tall. I tried to make my ants fly into an empty oatmeal canister, but it was a little too tall, so I cut it down to about eight inches.

I used denim to craft my first pair of little pants. Denim would be way too expensive to manufacture, but it would be fun to try and look cute. I made a paper pattern and asked one of the designers who could sew to make the pants, which we realized worked best as shorts. My little denim shorts were adorable! But we had to be cost effective and ended up making the pants out of molded bright blue plastic, with a pair of fire engine-red suspenders and big buttons to make them look spiffy. The legs were wide and sturdy, and the suspenders created an added challenge for players. The ants would often bounce off the suspenders and fall back onto the floor, making it more difficult than tiddlywinks. I wish I had kept the little denim pants, but I had no idea that my little ants would turn out to be one of the best-selling games in history and would still be for sale more than fifty years later.

Eugene and I designed and built the prototype so that it required no assembly, which was a huge plus when selling preschool games to manufacturers. The original instructions state the object of the game: "Have fun! Make your ants jump in the pants. Finish first and you'll be the winner!"

The first client who came for a presentation of my Ants in the Pants game was Herb Schaper in March of 1969. Herb was a burly, tall man and arrived at the meeting wearing, believe it or not, denim overalls.

Schaper Toys was a new client and our first from Minnesota. Herb Schaper, the founder, had started out as a postman but was also a tool and die maker. In 1949, he created Cootie, his first game, and by 1952 he had sold over a million units. His toy company was a huge success and I couldn't wait to show him Ants in the Pants.

Herb told us it was his first trip to Chicago, and we all went out to lunch before our presentation. While at the restaurant, Herb mentioned that he was a member of the John Birch Society, which I'd never heard of. I immediately learned that it was an ultraconservative, far-right, extremist organization. Marvin, on the other hand, was an extreme liberal who loved nothing more than a good argument. The lunch did not go well, but more than anything else, Marvin was a marvelous salesman and we soon focused on what mattered: selling the game to Schaper.

We got back to the office and the first game on the list was Ants in the Pants. When I eagerly unveiled the blue plastic shorts and sixteen brightly colored ants, Herb liked the game instantly and bought it on the spot. He refused to see any other products and told us to send him a contract for Ants in the Pants. It was the quickest sale in my forty-one years in the toy industry and the best one we ever had with Schaper.

Herb had already manufactured the game Don't Break the Ice, so he was familiar with the power and charm of idioms. He also recognized that it was a big advantage for him as the manufacturer and seller that the game required no assembly. Herb could easily manufacture the game on his injection-molding machine, which works by injecting heated liquid plastic into a mold that shapes the parts. It's an efficient and simple process. Herb took my prototype with him back to Minnesota and started preparing to manufacture it that year.

The game was a giant hit for Herb Schaper. Another toy company, Kusan, soon bought Herb's company. Kusan was eventually sold to Tyco, and in turn Tyco was sold to Mattel Inc. Mattel sold the Ants in the Pants game to Milton Bradley, which is now owned by Hasbro. Ants in the Pants really "jumped" around. But regardless of what toy company manufactured the game, MGA continued to receive royalty checks for its design. I invented Ants in the Pants in 1969 and it's still for sale today. It's sold millions of copies and continues to be played and loved by young children around the world.

During the months that I was designing Ants in the Pants, one day, out of the blue, Marvin called me into his office. He was smiling and I was surprised and thrilled when he told me he wanted to make me a partner. He told me that I'd no longer earn a salary but would get the partner's draw against company profits, which came in capital gains. I just nodded my head like I knew what he was talking about, but I'd received a D in accounting and failed economics. Marvin smiled and shook my hand and put his arm around me like a father. I thanked him profusely and left. I didn't have a clue what it all meant, but Marvin told me I would be making a lot more money. That part I got. After only eighteen months as a toy designer, I was made a partner, and the next great chapter in my career had begun.

About fifty years later, I was in Champaign visiting friends from the University of Illinois. One of them was the interim vice chancellor for academic affairs and provost, Edward Feser. When I told Ed I was working on my memoir, he told me a story. "When I was about five years old," he said, "I was sitting on Santa's lap at Christmastime. Santa asked me what I wanted for Christmas. I told him that I wanted Ants in the Pants. Santa didn't know about the preschool game and asked me why I would want to get any ants inside of my pants. He thought that was a strange request for a five-year-old." Santa Claus hadn't done his homework that year—he should have known all of the toys and games that were on sale each Christmas!

I had another wonderful gift in 1969 when Marlene gave birth to our first child, Marc, on June 11. I was delighted to be a father! Marlene gave up teaching to stay at home with Marc, and the three of us were a happy young family. Everything was going my way.

Chapter 8

My *Masterpiece* Is Born

M y creative juices flowed in a different direction after designing Ants in the Pants. My enduring love of art came to the fore and I dreamed about inventing a board game that would celebrate some of the greatest artists and paintings in history. My source of inspiration stood a mile away—one of the world's greatest museums, the Art Institute of Chicago.

I've always loved the Art Institute and went there frequently, particularly to study the French Impressionists. One of my favorite classes at the University of Illinois was art history. One day I was in the Art Institute gift shop, standing in the well-stocked postcard section, when I decided to buy one of each card that featured a famous painting. There were at least thirty different cards and probably more. An idea had struck me as I stood there studying the beautifully photographed postcards—I would invent a board game about buying and selling great works of art at auction. There were only a few times in my forty-one-year career when I saw a prototype game design and knew it would be a hit. One time was with my new board game—Masterpiece, the Art Auction Game.

Once I had the idea, the process of inventing the game was relatively easy. There are no hard-and-fast rules when it comes to inventing a board game. With Masterpiece, my first decision was that the time needed to play it had to be much shorter than for Monopoly, which takes way too long. I also decided that because the Monopoly board was square and used a square path, my Masterpiece board would be square but would use a round path instead.

The final board design was a gorgeous piece of art in its own right. Against a rich gold background, from the center of the board stared Rembrandt's stunning 1631 portrait, *Old Man with a Gold Chain*. Rembrandt's craggy-faced old man is dressed in a luxurious black cloak, a swashbuckling plumed beret, and a heavy gold chain around his neck. The gold chain was a great symbol for the game, since determining the winner was simple—whoever has the most money at the end of the game wins.

The original instructions from the 1970 version of Masterpiece show a photograph of an auctioneer standing on a stage displaying one of the famous paintings to the audience. The auctioneer looks out at the audience of buyers and the instructions begin,

> *"What am I bid?"*
>
> *Your favorite Van Gogh is on the auction block, and you are bidding for it against an array of eccentric art collectors and speculators.*
>
> *You want that Van Gogh painting. Should you up the bid to $5 million? $10 million? But what if it's a worthless forgery? You'll never know what it's really worth unless you outbid the competition. Keen observation, steady nerves, and a little luck make the difference in MASTERPIECE, an always exciting, sometimes risky excursion into the elite world of an international art auction.*

The gist of Masterpiece centered on buying and selling famous paintings at an art auction. As in the real world, the goal is to buy low and sell high. Each player acquired paintings and then traded with other players, negotiating and bluffing to get the best price. There were twenty-four cards of works of art by such artists as Monet, Degas, Renoir, Picasso, and Cezanne. Each painting card had on it the artist's name, the title, and a brief description of the painting. There were also twenty-four separate value cards that would be newly dealt each time you played the game, so the value of each painting changed every time you played.

At the beginning of play, both decks of cards would be shuffled and distributed to the players. Each player would paperclip two cards together—a painting card and, on the back of the painting card, a value card. After you acquired a painting, you would be able to secretly look at your card and see its value; unless you owned the painting, you weren't able to see its worth. Two of the value cards indicated the attached paintings were forgeries, and one value card was worth $1 million. What made the game extra fun was bluffing other players and trying to stick it to them while keeping a straight face.

While I was designing Masterpiece, I played it over and over and over with guys in the office. After each game session I would make incremental changes, tweaking the layout by adding more cash here or making it a bit luckier there. Designing games and toys is always a team effort, and I worked on its creation with graphic artists, model makers, and other designers. I played Masterpiece about a hundred times before I knew it was ready to sell to a manufacturer. The best formula for success was simple: when you're all done playing the game, you know you have a winner if someone says, "Let's play it again!"

Parker Brothers bought Masterpiece and one of their executives flew to Chicago to negotiate with the Art Institute for permission to reproduce their paintings. Parker Brothers proposed that the Art Institute of Chicago would earn a royalty on each game sold. For whatever reason, the Art Institute refused his offer, so he ended up making a deal with Boston's Museum of Fine Arts to portray their paintings instead.

From the beginning, Parker Brothers positioned Masterpiece to compete directly with Monopoly. They spent a fortune on a famous commercial. The scene opens at a fabulously opulent international art auction with a snooty auctioneer opening the bidding. Wealthy men and women issue bids, and then the scene shifts to something out of a James Bond movie. Instead of a crowd clustered around a poker table full of international spies and criminals, however, a chattering, drinks-laden throng focuses on a round table full of international art dealers and buyers. The narrator is a man with a deep voice and British accent. He drawls, "… the Masterpiece game calls for you to have nerves of steel, be an uncanny judge of people, and keep a stiff upper lip. Extraordinary game! Rich, tense, nerve-wracking." We see men in fabulously expensive suits wipe their brows; their monocles fall out of their eyes in surprise; and a heavily bejeweled woman screams in delight as she pulls a card from the table. Another man with a pencil mustache falls away from the table muttering, "Ruined, ruined." Over the top, the narrator says, "You can win the world's most treasured art collection or leave the auction a broken, naive ex-millionaire. Masterpiece—the greatest game since Monopoly!"

The television commercial worked. Parker Brothers sold 3.5 million units in its first five years, outselling Monopoly. Boston's Museum of Fine Arts received a nice royalty check from Parker Brothers. Masterpiece was updated and rereleased in 1976 and again in 1996.

In a 2019 *Good Housekeeping* article listing the most popular games for each year between 1960 and 1990, the magazine named Ants in the Pants as the winner of 1969 and recognized Masterpiece as 1970's champion. I was lucky enough to be the only toy inventor to twice earn the Good Housekeeping Seal of Approval.

But as productive as I was, I wasn't the only young new hotshot inventor hired by Marvin Glass in 1967. After Marvin employed me in April, he hired two other toy designers in November, Howard Morrison and Rouben Terzian. The three of us became great friends and business partners and, later, created a toy industry dynasty. When Marvin "discovered" us, Howard was thirty-three, Rouben was twenty-six, and I was twenty-four. The paths that led us to Marvin Glass were as random and varied as our personalities.

Howard Morrison grew up on the North Side of Chicago and graduated from the University of Wisconsin with a degree in electrical engineering. As a young man he worked for Underwriters Laboratories before getting into the toy business in the early 1960s. At Strombecke's Toys he focused on inventing electric road racing toys, which heavily influenced his later work. Howard, short with dark brown hair and a neatly trimmed beard and mustache, was a whiz at electro-mechanical work and electronic games.

Howard had an incredible sense of humor and saw the good in everyone. He was an energetic, funny designer who lit up every room he walked into. He talked to everyone and listened to their problems. He was a prolific inventor and more productive than Rouben and I put together. He invented toys, vehicles, games, ride-on toys, and, occasionally, dolls. He loved to do plush. He later went on to invent some of Glass's most important games and toys, including SSP Racers in 1970, Inchworm in 1971, and Simon in 1977. Howard generated the most income for Marvin Glass & Associates.

Rouben Terzian was Armenian and born in Beirut, Lebanon. He came to the United States when he was seventeen with the dream of pursuing a musical career as a violinist. Fortunately for us, he failed his music school audition. Rouben, a slender man with dark hair and wide sideburns, changed careers and studied industrial design at the Illinois Institute of Technology.

After he graduated, Rouben designed the interior for a Middle Eastern restaurant on the North Side of Chicago, Sayat Nova. Marvin Glass had dinner at the restaurant one night, was impressed with the design, and inquired who had done the work. Marvin found Rouben and offered him a job in November 1967, which he accepted immediately. Rouben was a gifted design engineer who loved to work on mechanical dolls. He created dolls that roller-skated, somersaulted, and danced. Some of his best-known dolls include Jumpsy, Upsy Baby, Movin' Groovin' Crissy, and Baby Skates.

Howard, Rouben, and I all did well early in our careers and were made partners within two or three years of being hired. One day, Marvin told all the partners that he would give $50,000 to the first partner who came up with an idea that generated $1 million in royalties for the company. Howard won.

In 1970, Howard created a revolutionary plastic toy race car, the SSP Racer, which stands for Super Sonic Power. Two things were new—the car didn't require a racetrack, and it didn't require batteries. Instead, a gyroscope powered the race car. A gyroscope is a heavy wheel that generates power when it spins at high speed.

Two parts came inside each toy box—the brightly painted, flashy race car, and a plastic rack gear, or stick, which Kenner dubbed the "T-Handled Power Stick." The power stick was an eighteen-inch-long, thin, flexible piece of plastic lined with gear teeth. To make it go, the child held the car in one hand and the power stick in the other. They first fed the stick through a slot in the center of the car so the teeth on the power stick engaged the teeth on the gyro—now it was poised for action. To engage the gyroscope and set it in motion, the child ripped out the power stick as fast as possible. The gyro screamed as it rotated at high speed, generating incredible power and turning the single rear tire. When the child set the car down on the sidewalk, driveway, or kitchen floor, it zoomed off at high speed until either bouncing off inanimate objects or coming to rest when the gyro's power was spent.

The original toy box proclaimed the SSP Racers to be the "World's Fastest BIG Racers.... Nothing Like 'Em! With *Super Sonic Power!*" The commercials advertised, "Those SSP Racers howl with power!" The colorful cars, designed to look like futuristic professional race cars or hot rods, had names like the King Cobra, Detonator, and Super Stalker. The kids and parents both loved toy. We licensed it to Kenner and made a fortune. Using a familiar business pattern, we created several popular offshoots of the original game, including Mini SSP Racer for younger kids and SSP Smash-Up Derby so kids could crash their cars and rebuild them on the spot.

As soon as Marvin wrote Howard a check for $50,000, Howard walked across the street to the Cosmopolitan Bank. He deposited $40,000 into his personal account and got $10,000 in hundred-dollar bills. Howard returned to the studio and passed out the bills to the model makers and designers who had helped him on the SSP Racer project. Howard is the kindest and most generous man I've ever known.

Soon after inventing his fabulous SSP Racers, Howard came up with another giant hit in 1971, the Inchworm ride-on toy for preschoolers. The child sat on a saddle like it was a miniature horse, but instead of four hooves, the Inchworm used a bounce-and-go motion with four wheels. We sold the idea to Hasbro, and a generation of little kids grew up bouncing their way down the sidewalks of America. Howard was a wonder.

Howard, Rouben, and I shared more than work through the years. We socialized together, vacationed together, and became best friends. We helped each other through our personal tragedies, including divorces and family deaths. We recognized each other's strengths and weaknesses. As designers, Howard's strength was producing electro-magnetic toys, Rouben's was creating dolls, and mine was developing games. We made a wonderful team, but we all knew that standing behind us was the chain-smoking, secretive, brilliant grandmaster himself, Marvin Glass.

Chapter 9

Mr. Machine and *Mouse Trap* Make It Big

M arvin Glass sent my professional imagination into overdrive. After working closely with him for several years, I understood that Marvin was a complicated, troubled genius. I've never met anyone like him. At first, I was reluctant to see him as anything but my boss, but he was almost thirty years older than I, and soon enough I loved him like a father. Marvin was my third mentor, which made me incredibly lucky. Some people never find even one.

Marvin Glass was born Marvin I. Goldberg on July 14, 1914, in Chicago. He was the only child of Louis Goldberg, who worked in the clothing industry, and Rose Glass. Marvin suffered an appallingly difficult childhood with a mother who was severely mentally ill. She tried to throw him out of a third-story window when he was six years old. For days on end, his mother tied him to a chair without food or water or being allowed to use a bathroom. Finally, when Marvin was eight and his mother was twenty-nine years old, she was committed to a mental institution where she remained until her death. Marvin's father was virtually absent. Marvin was taken in and raised by his mother's sister and her husband, where they lived in near poverty on the Southwest Side of Chicago near the Union Stock Yards.

Marvin dealt with his abusive childhood by escaping into his imagination, a place where he dreamed up and constructed new toys. He created a cardboard dog when he was four years old, but "I couldn't understand why I couldn't make the tail wag," he told the *Saturday Evening Post* in 1960. At eight, he built homemade Roman helmets, swords, and shields and played with them with his friends. "I always played Caesar and I never got assassinated," he told the *Post*. Sent away to military school in Wisconsin as a boy, he made friends by building scale models of Egyptian galleys and pirate ships. He constructed mock-ups of submarines that fired torpedoes and handcrafted tanks large enough to sit in. He hated military school and returned to Chicago.

A bright and gregarious teenager, Marvin set out to make money by selling encyclopedias when he was thirteen or fourteen. His later teenage years and early adulthood remain cloaked in mystery because he rarely told the same story twice about his chaotic and painful past. He later claimed to have graduated from the University of Chicago, but there is no record of him there as a student. As a young man, Marvin changed his last name to Glass to avoid anti-Semitism in the business world.

What is clear is that he got started as a toymaker at twenty-eight years old by selling a toy called the Tiny Town Theater in 1943. Marvin had a friend who designed animated window displays for a living, Joe Nudelman. A customer asked them to create a toy idea and the two men got to work. They developed an innovative design that enabled kids to insert and illuminate comic strips on their own personal film projector. In essence, they created a rudimentary precursor to the smartphones we all now carry.

Marvin and Nudelman earned $500 for their idea, but the manufacturer went on to earn $30,000 on the Tiny Town Theater. Marvin decided he would never again sell an idea without earning royalties on it. His decision eventually led him to earn fabulous wealth and personal fame, but not before a wild financial roller-coaster ride that lasted many years.

Marvin and Nudelman soon began working for a third friend, Judd Reed, who owned Reed Toys. Together they designed more toys that sold well, including animated paper cutout figures called Hingees. They obtained franchise agreements that allowed them to add characters like Mickey Mouse, Popeye, and Blondie to the Hingee line.

In 1944, Marvin bought out Nudelman and Reed and became president of Reed Toys. Marvin told the *Saturday Evening Post* in 1960 that he bought out his partners because they "didn't like customers. Sometimes they insulted them. I was always mercenary enough to be polite." Years later, one of Marvin's partners, Burt Meyer, explained it this way: "Marvin was very opportunistic and very forceful, much more forceful than Reed or Nudelman." Meyer added, according to the wonderful book *A World Without Reality: Inside Marvin Glass's Toy Vault!* by Bill Paxton: "Marvin was a very forceful sales guy. So he's going to get in there and make something—and he did."

Late in the 1940s, a young inventor named Edward Goldfarb walked through Marvin's door with a little cardboard box standing on two legs. When the box was pressed down, a mechanism hidden within the box caused a marble to fall out of the bottom. Marvin redesigned the cardboard box into a plastic chicken that would lay five eggs, one at a time, and sold the idea of the Busy Biddy chicken to Topic Toys of Chicago. Topic Toys sold 14,267,000 plastic chickens at 39 cents each in 1949. Marvin cleared $314,000 on the toy chickens after sharing royalties with Goldfarb. It was a mutually profitable relationship and both companies flourished. Marvin explained to the *Post* in 1960, "You know why they paid attention to the chicken? Everybody wanted to know where the marbles came from, that's what. They were like the circus clowns tumbling out of a jalopy." The advertisement for the sunshine yellow chicken called it "The adorable little chicken with the big personality." Edward Goldfarb became one of Marvin's key designers.

In 1948, when he was thirty-four years old, Marvin opened his own office space when he signed a lease for three rooms on the main floor of the Alexandria Hotel, a massive seven-story red brick building located at 57 E. Ohio Street. He had a reception room, his own office, and one workroom. He rented two other rooms in the hotel to live in. Though the neighborhood is now known as the trendy River North area, at that time it was a run-down, grimy section of town filled with seedy bars known as Rush Street. Hookers plied their trade out of the lounge at the Alexandria Hotel.

Marvin quickly made a fortune on the Busy Biddy chicken and other toys. Unfortunately, he promptly lost it. In 1949, he invested more than $1 million of his own money in the production of plastic, stained-glass-window Christmas ornaments. The windows were made with poor-quality plastic, and he advertised them late in the Christmas season. The ornaments bombed and Marvin fell $300,000 into debt. Friends, however, loaned him money to start over.

The 1950s were a pivotal decade for Marvin. He opened it mired in debt and married to his first wife. He ended the decade a wealthy man and in the process of divorcing his third wife, who was also his first wife. Marvin was thirty-four years old when he married his first wife, Dorothy, in 1948. The following year they had a daughter, Diana, but divorced in 1955. In 1957, Marvin married Phyllis Franz, who worked for Hugh Hefner at Playboy. They were divorced one year later. In 1959, when Marvin was forty-five, he remarried Dorothy, his first wife, but they divorced for the second time within a year. The list of wives just scratches the surface of Marvin's active love life, which he admitted always played second fiddle to his work.

Marvin made a lot of money in the 1950s by selling various toy dogs. He learned that toy dogs sold well, so he repeated the basic theme several times. In 1953, he designed Moody Mutt, a tan puppy that smiled until its paws were pushed down and then it scowled darkly. The Moody Mutt sold 3,600,000 units at 49 cents each and Marvin earned $64,000. The next year, he netted $38,000 with the Swimming Puppy, a white dog with black spots that rotated his legs and splashed in the bathtub. In 1956, he made $55,000 when he added Robo the Robot Dog, a square black dog with red ears that barked, wagged its tail, and walked. "Kids are imitators," Marvin told the *Saturday Evening Post* in 1960. "The thing that works as a toy is the commonplace that the child has seen before and can understand and manipulate."

Marvin's successful toys, however, weren't enough to bail him out of serious debt. The toy business was notoriously volatile and it was hard to borrow money from the banks. He borrowed money from everyone he could to meet his expenses, including payroll and machinery. Marvin was even rumored to have borrowed money from the mob in the mid-'50s.

Then Lady Luck shone on Marvin one day in the late 1950s when a wealthy car dealer who loved to gamble took an interest in him. Frank Katzin, a prosperous businessman who owned a Chevrolet dealership on the North Side of Chicago, became a major investor and part owner in Marvin Glass & Associates. Frank thought Marvin was a genius toy maker on the one hand, but a nut who couldn't handle money on the other. The two men constantly argued about money. Marvin told Frank he needed to spend more and Frank told Marvin he needed to spend less. Marvin always won. In the end, Katzin, who died in 1971, made a lot of money from Marvin Glass. For Marvin, Katzin's financial backing allowed him to stabilize MGA and turn it into the design juggernaut of the toy industry.

In the late 1950s, innovations in plastic and injection molding made it possible to inexpensively manufacture plastic parts. Marvin foresaw that cheap plastic would radically transform toy design, and he soon created a revolutionary product that would cement both his fortune and his legend—walking, talking plastic robots.

Marvin was forty-five years old in 1960, when he and his team of designers transformed the toy industry by inventing Mr. Machine, a transparent plastic robot man. The robot swung its arms and legs, talked, and wore a top hat. Fantastically, it was also like a Lego toy—children could build and dismantle it at will. When the new box was opened, the child saw forty-four plastic parts, a plastic wrench, and instructions. The child assembled the eighteen-inch-high red robot and set it in motion by turning a large wind-up screw on its back. Mr. Machine could walk forward or backward, turn around, and open his large jaw to say "ahh."

At first, it looked like Mr. Machine was destined to be an expensive flop. Marvin presented his invention to seven clients and they all said no. But Marvin had invested a lot of money in the robot's development and was desperate to sell his idea. He finally found a partner in Lionel Weintraub, the president of Ideal Toy. Lionel sorely needed a moneymaker and risked investing in Marvin's idea. Ideal Toys and Lionel spent a fortune on television commercials to promote Mr. Machine. Fortunately, their huge gamble paid off, and the walking robot became a highly profitable hit in 1960. In 1961, a *Time* magazine article described Marvin as "the Frankenstein who set Mr. Machine clunking and whirring through a million U.S. living rooms."

When Marvin saw the opportunity to repeat a best-selling toy in the 1960s, he embraced it, just like he had with his toy dogs the decade before. Mr. Machine was so profitable that Marvin immediately added technological advances to more of his plastic inventions. In 1961, he created Robot Commando, a nineteen-inch-tall, battery-powered "one-man army," complete with eyes that spun wildly. The child spoke into a microphone while twisting a knob and commanded the red and blue robot to move, swing its massive arms and fire rockets, or open up its top to shoot an extra-large missile. Robot Commando was another hit for Marvin and Lionel Weintraub.

In 1962, Marvin continued his pattern of developing a new twist on a good idea when he designed King Zor, a blue and green two-foot-long robot dinosaur. King Zor growled deeply, moved forward and back, and fired missiles at his enemies. In 1963, Marvin invented Dandy the Lion, an eighteen-inch-long tawny lion that stalked forward and backward, reared up on its hind legs, and roared.

Marvin's string of big hits continued when he invented one of the greatest games in history in 1963—Mouse Trap. It was one of the first plastic, mass-produced, three-dimensional games. Mouse Trap was a board game advertised as "zany action on a crazy contraption," in which players construct a Rube Goldberg-like mousetrap and attempt to trap their opponents' mouse-shaped game pieces. Both Parker Brothers and Milton Bradley turned down Mouse Trap, with the president of Milton

Bradley famously deriding the game as "a piece of plastic junk." Marvin again turned to Lionel Weintraub at Ideal Toy to make a deal. Ideal brought out Mouse Trap and it sold 1.2 million units in the first year. Mouse Trap continues to sell well today, more than fifty years later.

Starting with their deal for Marvin's concept of the Mr. Machine robot, Marvin and Lionel Weintraub changed the financial practices of the toy industry by perfecting the process of earning royalties for toy inventions. MGA earned 5 percent of the wholesale price on every product they sold. The manufacturer sets the wholesale price, and the retailer sets the retail price. The advantage of taking a percentage of the wholesale price instead of the retail price was twofold. First, sometimes retailers intentionally lowered the price of a hit toy and used it as a loss leader to get customers into the store, so the retail price might be lower than the wholesale price. Second, the price of toys increases over time. When a toy sold for many years and its price increased, MGA continued to earn 5 percent of the new wholesale price. MGA and its partners earned millions on toys with a long shelf life. They continue to earn money from licensing agreements on games that still sell today, such as Operation, Ants in the Pants, Mouse Trap, and Simon.

As a young man, Marvin learned business from the school of hard knocks when two toy ideas were stolen from him before he could profit off them. He never forgot the bitter lesson he learned, and from then on, he patented every idea that was developed by his studio, even if the product didn't hit the market. He energetically fought any attempt to steal his inventions. As early as 1949, Marvin and Topic Toys defended the patent on the Busy Biddy chicken and forced a copycat to immediately cease production. "We Stand Ready to Act as Strenuously Against Anyone Else Who Might Infringe," crowed a 1949 advertisement for Topic Toys. Marvin had a patent lawyer to file his paperwork and monitor the world for any theft of his toys and games.

Before Marvin Glass & Associates became a powerhouse, few toy manufacturers would look at design ideas from outside toy designers. Almost every accomplished toy designer worked at an in-house studio. Now, top executives from manufacturers such as Hasbro, Milton Bradley, and Mattel flew to Chicago to see what new ideas Marvin had in his back pocket.

Marvin also insisted that MGA be allowed to audit clients' books. While there were occasional disagreements on the figures, MGA never went into litigation with a client. Clients paid like clockwork, four times a year. MGA never lost customers. There's always a big demand for the latest inventions, because kids have to have new choices every Christmas. And year in and year out, MGA designed highly profitable toys.

Another revolution hit the toy industry around the same time as the switch to plastic toys—television advertising. In 1955, Disney's *Mickey Mouse Club* was broadcast into living rooms around the country, and a mass audience of children was born. Children became their own decision makers, and advertisers spoke directly to them instead of going through their parents. Now, children asked their parents for toys they had seen on TV.

Marvin Glass quickly became adept at television advertising. "We could now go directly to the kids, and that meant everything," Marvin told *Time* magazine in 1962. "Most Glass toys embody several principles: 1) they are big (so they participate with a child); 2) they are made of plastic, with all of plastic's build-in obsolescence; 3) they are eminently TV-promotable. I believe toys should serve no purpose other to entertain a child…. We were selling dreams."

The royalty money poured in. In 1962, Marvin used his wealth to finally build the home he never had. He bought and had rebuilt a dilapidated coach house just two blocks from Lake Michigan at 1319 Forest Avenue in Evanston. Designed by famed architect Joseph Silsbee, a mentor to Frank Lloyd Wright, the house was originally built in 1894 as a coach house for a massive stone mansion that was owned by grain dealer William Bartlett.

Marvin hired an architect to repair the original exterior and completely redesign and rebuild the interior. The architect, Jim Stewart, gutted the structure and created a four-bedroom, 5,000-square-foot house with a custom outdoor swimming pool. A sauna and hot tub were added in the basement. The house faced west, and its elegant, original cobblestone courtyard still exists. It took Stewart more than a year to complete the work, but in 1964, Marvin moved into his luxurious house. He loved it and lived there happily for the rest of his life.

Marvin married his fourth wife, Diane Bosun, a Playboy Bunny, in 1962. They divorced one year later, but through Diane, Marvin met Elizabeth Roberts, a *Playboy* centerfold. Marvin and Elizabeth met in 1964, when he was fifty and she was twenty-three years old. They never married, but Elizabeth became an on-again, off-again live-in girlfriend for two years. Marvin enjoyed life at his new home, and soon changed his place of business as well.

In 1965, Marvin was forced to move out of his office space at the Alexandria Hotel when the building was sold. He bought a 10,000-square-foot building and moved the company several blocks west and north to 815 N. LaSalle Street, just across from the Moody Bible Institute. With the help of an architect, Marvin gutted the west-facing brick edifice and renovated the space into a fabulous facility, complete with first-rate machinery and two model shops for the model makers, personal office space for the toy designers, and a luxurious conference room. Marvin's own spectacular office was outfitted with a 500-gallon fish tank, a genuine signed Tiffany chandelier, and an original Chagall on the wall behind his desk.

By 1967, when Marvin was fifty-two years old, he had built the most successful independent toy design company in the world. It was into this flourishing business that I was hired in April of that year.

Chapter 10

Marvin Glass, Superstar

O ne of the first things that hit me upon being hired was Marvin's extreme concern with security and protecting his ideas. Marvin required all of our clients to sign a nondisclosure agreement before they were allowed to see any of our inventions. Some toy companies refused to work with Marvin Glass because they balked at signing our NDA. But money talked, and over the years we made a lot of money for toy manufacturers, so more and more companies agreed to sign our NDA in order to see our patented creations, including Milton Bradley, Fisher-Price, Hasbro, Ideal Toy, Parker Brothers, and Mattel.

Our NDA was only two pages long. The first page was standard legal language. When the client flipped to the second page, however, he saw only the blank back of a photograph. The client had to sign and date the back of the photograph before he was allowed to detach it from the page and turn it over to look at the picture of the proposed toy or game. Written on the page underneath the photo was the description of the invention. This process was typical of Marvin's secrecy and wariness.

When looked at against the rest of the toy industry in the 1960s, Marvin's business practices made sense. In 1963, Milton Bradley was doing $17 million in sales, but by 1968 they were bringing in almost triple that amount, $45 million a year. In 1968, Glass-designed toys accounted for $11 million, or 26 percent, of their income, according to a 1968 *Coronet* magazine article. Ideal Toy Company had gone from $17 million to $49 million with Glass toys. Schaper Toys rose from $3 million to $9 million, with Glass items accounting for 30 percent of their increased sales. "The biggest toy firm, Mattel, sells $150 million in products with a staff of 10,000. Our output and intake are second in the industry with a staff of 50," Marvin told the *Evening and Sunday Times* in 1968. "Outside of Mattel, we set most of the trends. I hate to sound immodest, but it's a fact." Marvin Glass & Associates was a toy industry juggernaut.

Before I started working for Marvin in 1967, I knew from reading the 1960 *Saturday Evening Post* article that he was an unusual man. My awareness of Marvin's eccentricities helped me navigate my first year as a toy designer, when it would never have occurred to me that Marvin and I would become both business partners and close friends. But within two years of starting at MGA, I realized that our relationship was more than just that of employer and employee. Marvin had come to think of me as the son he never had. He had three daughters but no sons. Marvin always treated me kindly and with respect. It helped that I was producing an endless supply of prototype games that we showed to clients. For me, inventing games and toys was fun, not work. I loved working for Marvin, and I began to know him not just as my boss but as a man.

Just weeks after my first son was born, in June 1969, Marvin took all of the partners up to the recently opened Playboy Club in Lake Geneva, Wisconsin, about ninety minutes north of Chicago. Marvin said we were there to think about toy ideas, but I think he wanted to check out the new club with his seven men for company. A Bunny waited on us at dinner. When this gorgeous woman came to take our drink order, Marvin put his hand around her waist, complimented her profusely, and asked, "How would you like to come to work for me in Chicago?" She immediately answered, "Yes," which surprised the hell out of everyone,

Ants in the Pants, designed in 1968 for Marvin Glass and Associates (MGA) and licensed by Schaper Toys, is still on the market today. In 1969, it was the first of two of Breslow's games to earn the Good Housekeeping "Game of the Year" award.

ANTS IN THE PANTS® & ©2021 Hasbro, Inc. Used with permission.

Breslow's first game design at MGA, introduced by Milton Bradley in 1967.

BUCKET OF FUN® & ©2021 Hasbro, Inc. Used with permission.

Masterpiece, introduced in 1970 by Parker Brothers, was the second game designed by Breslow and MGA to earn the Good Housekeeping "Game of the Year" award.

MASTERPIECE® & ©2021 Hasbro, Inc. Used with permission.

The Evel Knievel Stunt Cycle was created by MGA and Ideal Toys and introduced in 1973. MGA met and signed up Evel Knievel and built the articulated figure to hang on to Ideal's fabulous gyro motorcycle. The combination of Ideal's motorcycle and MGA's Evel character is what made the success of this toy.

The blockbuster hit Simon was designed by Howard Morrison at MGA and introduced in 1978 by Milton Bradley.

Hot Wheels Criss-Cross Crash debuted in 1979 and was a huge hit for Mattel and MGA.

In 1978, Post Office Telecommunications introduced the Mickey Mouse phone, designed by Howard Morrison at MGA.

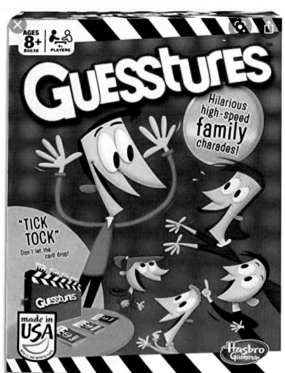

Milton Bradley debuted the Breslow designed game, Guesstures, in 1990. A giant version of the BMT game was often played on The Ellen DeGeneres Show.

Created by BMT, Mattel premiered My Size Barbie in 1992.

Mattel introduced Fashion Polly Pocket in 1999, using a new fabric created by designers at BMT.

Breslow designed the Trump Game at BMT in 1988 and traveled to Trump Tower in NYC with his partner Rouben Terzian to pitch the game to Mr. Trump. Breslow went back for a second meeting with Mr. Trump to make the "deal." Milton Bradley introduced the game in 1989.

Jeffrey Breslow at his high school graduation in 1960. The photographer told him not to smile.

Marvin Glass in 1960.

Jack Klugman, Anson Isaacson, Tony Randall, and Jeffrey Breslow at the New York Toy Fair in 1975.

Kathy Dunn, 1943 to July 27, 1976

Breslow and Carol Channing at a New York Super Simon party in 1980.

Jeffrey, Howard, and Rouben founded Breslow, Morrison, and Terzian in 1988. In 2003, they changed their company name to Big Monster Toys.

Breslow in 2011 with his sculpture of a swinging boy in bronze with a maple tree section and granite base. The sculpture has a permanent home at the University of Chicago, Comer Children's Hospital.

Edward Zagorski's first selfie with Jeffrey at the University of Illinois in 2013.

Pablo Atchugarry, Nando Parrado, and Jeffrey in Punta del Este, Uruguay for the dedication of Jeffrey's sculpture, MIAGRO EN LOS ANDES (Miracle in the Andes), in March 2022.

Twenty-two years ago Jeffrey became close friends with Nando Perrado, one of the two young men who hiked down the mountain and saved his friends seventy-two days after the crash of the Uruguayan airplane on October 13, 1972. Their friendship inspired Jeffrey's sculpture, which is dedicated to the crash victims. Sixteen stones affixed to the giant boulder represent those who survived. The smaller stones atop the steel rods represent the twenty-nine people who died. The steel rods sway in the wind.

Uruguay, Jeffrey with ten of the survivors from the plane crash, March 2022.

including Marvin. A few weeks later, Nancy, the former Playboy Bunny, was working next to Pauline as the second receptionist at our toy studio. That was Marvin.

The Playboy Club had a pool table, and I asked Marvin if he wanted to shoot a game. He said he had never played, and I offered to show him how to hold a cue and play. I had learned to play pool in high school when my brother Gene and I saved up our earnings and our dad let us buy a pool table for the basement. As it turned out, Marvin was uncoordinated. He didn't take well to the game but said he loved playing. His next words shocked me—he wanted to build a special room right off his dining room for his new pool table. "What new pool table?" I asked. "You're going to find me an antique pool table," Marvin replied.

Shopping with an unlimited budget was lots of fun. I found a spectacular antique Brunswick table for $4,000. Within six months, the room addition was finished and the table was installed. I shot pool many times in Marvin's billiard room, where some of his dinner guests would retire for cigars and brandy after a delicious Chinese meal prepared by Poy Tom, Marvin's personal chef. I never again saw Marvin lift a pool cue.

It was a day in January 1970 that Marvin told me he was being honored as the Toy Man of the Year by the British International Toy Industry. He asked me to join him on his upcoming trip to Brighton, England, a seaside resort ninety minutes south of London. I was excited because I'd never been to Europe, but I knew the winter weather would be brutal on the southern coast of England.

Marvin only flew first class, and I was delighted when I learned I'd also be flying first class for the first time. But my coworkers smiled and joked when they heard I was flying with Marvin. They told me he was deathly afraid of flying. I didn't know what they meant until I got to the airport and saw Marvin. He was sweating profusely and looked awful. I was shocked at Marvin's appearance and equally shocked when he introduced me to his psychiatrist. He told me the doctor would accompany us on the flight to England and back. I forget the psychiatrist's name, but I'll call him Dr. Pill Popper.

Marvin and Dr. Popper sat in the row behind me, with Marvin at the window and the doctor on the aisle. I was on the aisle, and it seemed every time I turned around, the doctor was popping another pill into Marvin's mouth. I couldn't watch. When we landed at Heathrow, Marvin was unconscious and had to be taken off the plane on a stretcher. Fortunately, we arrived in England a few days early because Marvin knew he would need time to recover from the flight.

Marvin had to give a speech on the night he received his award and he was nervous about it, but he spoke well and was warmly received by the British toy industry executives. The next day we drove to London in a private limo, which Marvin kept for the whole trip. We stayed at Claridge's, a five-star palatial hotel in the Mayfair district that has a long-standing connection to English royalty. We went to the theater and saw many sights, including the British Museum, Piccadilly Circus, and the Tower of London. I fell head over heels in love with London and later attended the British toy fair many times.

By this time, Marvin's fame as a sensational businessman and eccentric and colorful womanizer was national news. His parties had become legendary and he was friendly with Hugh Hefner. In May 1970, *Playboy* featured Marvin in a full-length article titled "A Playboy Pad: Swinging in Suburbia, an imaginative toy designer turns a staid old carriage house into a focal point for fun and games." The article featured Marvin and his spectacular house in Evanston, describing it as "a personalized approach to creating a live-in adult toy." There were sixteen photos of Marvin, his house and original artwork, and the Bunnies. Marvin was in two of them, one in his living room and one in the dining room. Another photo showed four Playmates sipping champagne in Marvin's Jacuzzi, described as an "emperor-sized ceramic Roman tub for eight."

Marvin's party scene exploded. Mel Taft, Milton Bradley's vice president of research and development, remembered how things changed after the *Playboy* article. "Nobody from Marvin Glass or from the outside was [at the *Playboy* shoot], and that night they had a party. I guess a pretty wild party," Taft said. "People like myself were scared to death for fear that he would get too much publicity and that all our wives at home would be saying, 'Oh, so that's what you were up to at Marvin Glass.' Fortunately, that never happened." Mel, a tall, slender man with dark hair who wore a crew cut and a beaming smile his entire life, was one of MGA's best clients and a great friend. He loved playing games and acting like a kid—for decades he happily got down on the floor and tested prototypes with us. Mel was also a frequent visitor at Marvin's parties.

Alison Katzman, hired in 1971 as one of the first women toy designers at MGA, recalled how clients partied at Marvin's house: "[T]hey were all trying to impress each other on how important each one of them was to the toy business and, of course, Marvin would try to outdo them all. He would put on a show that was really special and he loved the drama.... He loved the excitement of being a big tycoon, toy mogul, and he...liked his parties. When some of the big clients came into town he would wine and dine them and supply the female entertainment."

About a month after the *Playboy* article appeared, Pauline paged me over the loudspeaker and asked me to come to the front desk. I wondered if I'd done something wrong and was relieved when she told me Marvin wanted Marlene and me to come for dinner on Friday night. I'd never been to his house and Marvin hadn't met Marlene yet. She hadn't even been to my office, primarily because she had a teaching job in Skokie that kept her busy during the day. Even if Marlene had come to visit my office, she could only have seen the front reception area. The back studio was off-limits to everyone, including family. The wives and girlfriends weren't happy about that. Sometimes I felt like I worked for the CIA or FBI.

Marlene was delighted at the invitation and asked, "How many people are going to be there?" "Maybe three or four," I guessed. When the evening arrived, we bought a bottle of wine and drove our brown, 1965 four-door Chevy Biscayne to Marvin's house. As a toy designer, I may have been a hotshot, but my car was not.

When we pulled up, we saw that Marvin's old coach house had a stone circular driveway and a small Fernando Botero sculpture in front. Cars were already parked out front and we realized that the dinner was bigger than we'd expected. We walked past the outdoor swimming pool, lined on two sides by beautiful multicolored canvas cabanas. Marvin's house resembled a small summer resort. We looked at each other and said, "WOW!" and we hadn't even gotten through the door yet. The imposing wooden front door had an ornate knocker and no doorbell. We knocked and a tuxedo-clad butler opened the door. The sound of music, laughter, and clinking glasses filled the air as we walked in. Marlene and I turned to each other again and silently mouthed, "WOW!"

My guess had been way off. There were twenty-five or thirty people inside. We hadn't expected a quiet Friday night Shabbat dinner with candles, but we also hadn't expected a huge party. In the corner was a three-piece band, the same group that had performed at our wedding two years earlier. We were the youngest guests and I was shocked when I realized I was the only one from work. I didn't know anyone but Marvin.

Marvin graciously chatted with Marlene, who was short and petite with lovely dark hair and soft green eyes. Marvin, with my beautiful wife clinging to his arm, happily escorted us through his magnificent art collection. I recognized an original Salvador Dali painting in his dining room and an original Picasso and a small, original Renoir in the living room. I was blown away with the quality and quantity of artwork that filled his home; it must have cost a small fortune. Later that evening we enjoyed a superb Chinese buffet prepared by Poy Tom. It was a spectacular evening and my first real insight into this remarkable man.

Marvin's dinner invitation was a fabulous reward for my fast start at work. Bucket of Fun was under contract with Milton Bradley, and I had several other promising projects in the pipeline, including the Big Mouth game and Who You game. I loved working for Marvin and didn't want to jeopardize our relationship. I knew some other toy designers were jealous of my quick success, so I never revealed to anyone at work that Marlene and I enjoyed dinner at Marvin's house with his personal friends.

Now that Marvin was comfortably situated in his gorgeous home, he decided in 1971 that it was time to expand the studio at 815 N. LaSalle

Street. A few years earlier, he had purchased a second building adjoining the original 10,000-square-foot building. The newer building was only one story, and while it added 5,000 square feet, it remained separate and under its own roof. Marvin hired an architect to join the two buildings into one structure. The architect added a second story to the newer building and covered it all under one roof, giving the studio a total of 20,000 square feet. Pursuant to Marvin's orders, there were no windows in the building, so that spies couldn't infiltrate and steal his designs. The architect finished the project by adding a limestone façade to the entire structure. Shortly afterward, Marvin leased land on the north side of the building and added a sixty-car parking lot.

In keeping with his innate paranoia and secretiveness, Marvin added state-of-the-art electronic security to his new facility. Visitors were confronted with multiple locked doors, buzzers, intercoms, and security cameras everywhere. Every internal door closed and locked automatically, preventing employees from wandering around and seeing what other employees were working on. Marvin's intense need for security was just one of his many oddities. He also developed an unusually serious outlook on the toy business.

Marvin's philosophy on the vital importance of toys for children evolved over time. "If only people would select toys for a child with the same care that the parents select a dentist for him! After all, a dentist works only on his teeth, but a toy works on his imagination and helps shape his whole life," Marvin told the *Plymouth Traveler* in 1961.

None of Marvin's opinions changed as profoundly as his philosophy on toy guns. Marvin's gun designs sold extremely well early in his career. He noticed that Mattel, boosted by TV advertising, sold millions of expensive toy guns in the mid-1950s. Television broadcast a heavy dose of cowboy and Western shows, including *Gunsmoke, Have Gun-Will Travel,* and *The Rifleman.* Little boys pretended to be cowboys and lawmen, and so did little girls. Marvin took advantage of his audience's fascination and invented many profitable toy guns, including the Fastest Gun by Kilgore in 1958, the Marx Man Ricochet Carbine by Marx in 1959, and the Secret Rifle cap gun by Hubley in 1960.

The Holy Grail of toy manufacturing in those years was a toy gun that could emit a sound like the ricochet sound on television. *Bing-bing-bing!!* No one could produce the right sound. Many toy manufacturers worked feverishly on the project, but finally, after two years and thousands of dollars, Marvin got there first. When Marvin presented his Ric-O-Shay cap pistol to a large group of skeptical executives, they spontaneously broke into applause when Marvin pulled the trigger.

Marvin sold his Ric-O-Shay cap pistol to Hubley Toys in 1959. It sold more than one million guns in the first eight months and earned a fortune for both companies. Marvin strongly supported toy guns then, "because you can take away a fellow's cap gun, but not the aggression he takes out with it. Small boys need to make a big noise," he told UPI in 1961.

Marvin changed his mind when president John F. Kennedy was assassinated on November 22, 1963. After that, he hated toy guns. He never designed another one. "A toy gun is made to pretend that one is killing," Marvin told the *Chicago Tribune* in 1968. "A manufacturer has the responsibility not only to profits, but also to the mental health and character of children. Realistic guns, advertised realistically, convey the idea that violence is a legitimate persuader. The toy gun may be the ingredient that sets in motion another potential assassin." Marvin made a public appeal to manufacturers to end toy gun production. He held that strict belief for the rest of his life.

Marvin controlled every part of the business. He always reviewed Harry Disko's list the day before a client presentation, often deciding at the last second before closing that we didn't have enough new products to pitch. Marvin had no family to go home to at night, and he sometimes convened a 6:00 p.m. meeting of key partners to think up just one more idea for the next day's presentation.

The first time this happened to me, my idea was picked and I had to pull an all-nighter, which I hadn't done since my college days. Marvin left the studio around midnight and wished Eugene and me luck at finishing our prototype. We called our game Hero Mouse and it involved moving four little plastic mice around a board, but it was too expensive to produce and we never sold it. Nonetheless, Eugene and I had a lot of fun building the prototype in one night, although I experienced a major surprise.

Around 1:00 a.m., I was shocked to hear Marvin screaming naval commands through the building's PA system—"Full speed ahead," "Take no prisoners," and so on. Eugene explained that Marvin had the phone company install a unique line from his house to the studio speakers back in the late '60s. That way, we could hear his voice as he shouted encouraging words through the studio speakers from his home phone. Marvin was an intense, driven businessman and eccentric genius, but he wasn't the only one I worked with in the toy business.

Chapter 11

The *Evel Knievel Stunt Cycle* Takes Off

Many of our employees were more than a little odd. Case in point was Lyle Conway, who worked for Marvin Glass as a sculptor from 1972 to 1976. Lyle graduated from the Art Institute of Chicago sometime in the late '60s. Marvin hired him as a sculptor to work on dolls, animals, and figures. We soon realized that Lyle was way too talented for us, and I was sure he would move onto a much bigger stage, which he did.

Lyle reported to Marvin and Harry Disko, not to me, but after his first two weeks on the job, I called him into my office to ask him a personal question. Lyle had worn an identical green corduroy shirt and green corduroy pants every day. He didn't smell bad and his clothes weren't dirty, but I was curious, so I asked him, "Don't you have any other clothes?" We didn't have a dress code, but I thought that wearing the same outfit every day was weird and made him stand out to the other employees.

Lyle, a tall, stocky man with thick brown hair and a beard, explained that he owned seven green corduroy shirts and seven pairs of green corduroy pants. They all hung in his closet. He had no other clothes, and that way he didn't have to decide what to wear when he got up in the morning. He told me he had seven outfits because he did laundry once a week. He wore heavy army boots so you couldn't see his socks, and I certainly didn't inquire about his underwear. I said, "OK." Lyle was ahead of his time on the concept of decision fatigue that later became the mark of some successful businessmen.

Lyle would sometimes goof around during the day and then stay up all night working on a deadline. The next morning, his results were spectacular. Marvin Glass & Associates had elaborate Halloween parties, and designers would work all year on costumes, often on company time. We finally abandoned the Halloween parties in the mid-'80s because they cost too much and employees spent too much time designing Halloween costumes and not enough time designing toys. In 1976, however, Lyle and his girlfriend stole the show at one memorable event.

Lyle and his girlfriend came to the Halloween party that year dressed as two ape characters from *Planet of the Apes*. Lyle had sculpted ape heads and costumes that were as good as the movie characters'. At the party, the two of them squatted and made ape sounds the entire evening and never came out of character. No one could identify who was inside the costumes by looking at them, but we knew one of them had to be Lyle because only he could have made those spectacular ape getups. It could not have been anyone else.

When Lyle left us sometime in the mid-'70s, he went to work for Frank Oz, who worked on *Sesame Street* with Jim Henson. Frank Oz created the characters of Bert, Grover, and Cookie Monster. Lyle Conway found the perfect fit for his exceptional talent.

In 1986, I was in the movie theater watching a Christmas release of Frank Oz's *Little Shop of Horrors* with Rick Moranis, Vincent Gardenia, Steve Martin, Bill Murray, and John Candy. This hilarious movie was made years before computer animation was invented. The gigantic moving plant, Audrey II, was actually constructed by using a series of animated puppets. At the end of the film, Lyle's name popped up on the screen as special effects creator of Audrey II. Lyle was nominated for an Academy Award for special effects that year and enjoyed a successful Hollywood career. It was fabulous working with such a talented man at MGA, but we always knew he was destined for greater things. I don't know if Lyle ever bought different clothes.

Another extraordinary person that Marvin and I came to know well and prosper with was Evel Knievel, the legendary showman and stunt motorcycle rider. We met him in 1973 when he came to Chicago to perform one of his death-defying motorcycle jumps at the Chicago International Amphitheatre. Evel was born Robert Craig Knievel in 1938 in Butte, Montana. He grew up as a rough motorcycle kid whose original nickname was Evil, but he changed the spelling because he didn't want to be thought of as an outlaw motorcycle gang member.

Knievel rocketed into stardom in 1967 with his failed motorcycle jump over the fountains in front of Caesars Palace hotel in Las Vegas. His motorcycle lost power as he hit the takeoff ramp and he came up short on the landing ramp. He tumbled over and over, broke multiple bones, and suffered a concussion. He spent thirty days in the hospital, but his reputation as a fearless daredevil started to grow exponentially.

Evel was savvy enough to have had the entire jump filmed at his own expense by his own crew. He ultimately sold the film to ABC-TV for a lot of money. When ABC ran the film, Knievel became an instant national star, more because of his spectacular crash and survival than the actual jump. Evel Knievel had hit upon a new kind of entertainment—the real-life, death-defying exhibitionist. His motorcycle jump stunts and crashes became increasingly famous, and by 1973, Knievel was one of the biggest celebrities in the country.

Marvin Glass & Associates had never before ventured into the licensing of living people or cartoon characters. The concept of making a preschool toy with Mickey Mouse or a toy gun under license with the Lone Ranger was not in Marvin's vision. He thought our toys were strong enough on their own merit. Marvin hated the idea of licensing real people to his toys, but a friend of his knew Evel Knievel and convinced Marvin to meet with him.

In late March 1973, Evel was in Chicago for a motorcycle jump at the International Amphitheatre, and Marvin and I went to watch. It was brutal, but afterward Marvin invited Evel to his house for a meeting and asked me to come too. We waited a long time for Evel to show up that night.

Finally, Evel arrived at Marvin's house wearing his trademark gala costume—a white jumpsuit adorned with a blue V with white stars on his shirt and along his pants. Always a showman, he even topped it off with a red, white, and blue cape! He stood about six feet tall with a full head of sandy brown hair, long sideburns, a square chin, and cool sunglasses. Evel was a handsome, dashing figure who resembled a superhero more than a motorcycle guy. He looked like he had just stepped from the pages of a comic book. Here was a man who knew about presentation—a real-life superstar!

Fortunately, Marvin found Evel to be fascinating, not ridiculous. Marvin immediately signed him to an exclusive deal for all rights to toys, games, and other licensed products, even though we didn't have a single toy idea in mind. Marvin matched Evel's showmanship by telling him what we were going to do for him. Marvin could pitch with the best and didn't need a cape. Marvin persuaded Evel and me that we were going to earn a fortune together, and we did just that.

Marvin had finally met his match. Here was a man as dynamic, publicity-savvy and imaginative as he was. Thankfully, Marvin was smart enough to see it and embrace it rather than fight it. Evel Knievel understood how to market himself. He knew he was his own product. Evel was a living superhero sitting in Marvin's living room. And you gotta love his name. If it had been Sam Schwartz jumping motorcycles, it wouldn't have worked.

Marvin Glass & Associates initially produced several Evel Knievel toys and games, but none were memorable. Marvin then invited Lionel Weintraub, the president of Ideal Toy, to come in for an Evel presentation.

Lionel came, but the meeting fell flat—he had no idea who Evel Knievel was or what he did. Our presentation was a bust. We felt like we were pitching Superman and the client had asked, "Who the hell is Superman?"

When Lionel got home to New York, however, he told his son, Rich, an executive at Ideal, about our presentation. Rich Weintraub knew all about Evel jumping rows of cars on his motorcycle. Rich had seen the ABC fiasco in front of Caesars Palace in Vegas and was a huge fan of the daredevil motorcyclist. Happily, Lionel listened to his son, changed his mind, and jumped on the Evel Knievel bandwagon. MGA, Ideal, and Evel Knievel all went on to make millions by working together.

Unbeknownst to us, Ideal Toy had just developed a fabulous toy motorcycle. It was acrobatic, loud, and super-fast, no batteries required. The player loaded the bike into a wind-up crank launcher that was energized by hand-turning a wheel. The harder you cranked, the faster the wheel turned and the louder the toy screamed. When you stopped cranking and released it, the motorcycle shot off like a noisy rocket. What made it incredible, though, was a uniquely designed internal gyroscope that kept the bike upright and enabled it to do dazzling flips and spins. The bike popped wheelies, performed somersaults, and sailed over high jumps while still retaining its balance. But Ideal had no rider for its motorcycle!

MGA solved Ideal's problem—one Ideal didn't even recognize they had. We invented an articulated model motorcycle rider that looked just like Evel. He sported flowing blond hair, wore his signature outfit, and protected his head with a blue helmet. Our adjustable Evel Knievel toy could bend his arms, legs, and torso in dozens of different ways, and even be positioned to ride his bike upside down or backward if you wanted him to. The rider was attached securely to the motorcycle and always stayed on the bike, which was more than the real Evel did during many of his jumps.

The Evel Knievel Stunt Cycle was a smash hit when it was released before Christmas in 1973. No one could keep it in stock. If you were a boy living in the United States in the early 1970s, you owned and played with an Evel Knievel motorcycle stunt set. If you didn't have one, you desperately wanted one. Maybe your friend had one. That's how popular the toy was. Kids raced their bikes against each other and built their own obstacle courses and jumps. They crashed their Evel motorcycles repeatedly and rejoiced when they always got up for more. The toys entertained kids for hours. By combining Ideal's dynamic motorcycle with MGA's rider, we created a toy phenomenon. But as gigantic as the toy was when it debuted in 1973, it was about to become even bigger.

In 1968, before we met Evel, he started a crazy rumor that he was going to jump his motorcycle over the Grand Canyon. The U.S. government said no, and he wasn't allowed to jump on federal land. Eventually, Evel was able to lease private land in the Snake River Gorge in southern Idaho for his dramatic canyon jump, scheduled for September 8, 1974.

ABC Sports was unwilling to pay the huge amount Evel wanted for the live television rights, so he hired a private production company to broadcast his jump in movie theaters and on closed-circuit TV. MGA chartered a private, forty-seat twin-prop plane to fly people to Idaho to watch the jump. I wasn't interested in going to Idaho—I had two young sons and didn't feel comfortable flying on a chartered plane just to watch a few minutes of insanity. I stayed in Chicago and managed the studio.

Evel knew that he couldn't possibly jump the yawning canyon on a motorcycle, so he constructed a steam-powered rocket that was large enough for him to sit in. He built a high, steep steel ramp on one side of the canyon. He had the rocket, which he named the Skycycle X-2, mounted at the base of the steel ramp. When it was showtime, he was lowered into the Skycycle by a crane. A clear cowling closed him in before the rocket was fired.

Evel's jump was a disaster. A few seconds after takeoff, a technological error caused the rocket's parachute to mistakenly deploy, causing it to decelerate. The Skycycle X-2 went into a nosedive and headed straight toward the rushing river. Fortunately, the parachute caught on some trees growing out of the side of the cliff and the rocket slowed before it finally crashed into the sandy riverbank. If the Skycycle had landed in the Snake River, Evel would have drowned. He wore a harness and had no plan for getting out of the rocket unaided. Evel's only injury was a broken nose.

Disaster or not, all of the publicity generated by Evel's close brush with death made him an even bigger superstar. In the entertainment world, hype is essential. Public relations and marketing are crucial. The fact that Evel Knievel was a real motorcycle rider and daredevil added enormously to the commercial appeal of our toys.

You can promote the hell out of a movie, television show, book, or toy, but you can't turn a lousy product into a winner; it has to succeed by word of mouth from others who loved it. To be successful, your commodity has to be a great product. And the Evel Knievel Stunt Cycle set with the motorcycle, figure, and wind-up crank launcher was a fabulous toy that delivered all it promised when it was introduced. With no batteries to wear out, it was durable and great fun for continuous play. The internal gyroscope kept it running straight and true. Just as advertised, it could flip over obstacles, run down stairs, and always right itself. Both Ideal and MGA supplied great concepts with fabulous execution to the Evel Knievel Stunt Cycle, and it paid off.

Evel Knievel was so hot that we put his image on every product we could think of, including lunch boxes, bubble gum, wastebaskets, pajamas, and more games. Ideal quickly manufactured the Evel Knievel Stunt Stadium, Scramble Van, Hobby Kit, Canyon Sky Cycle, and more. Evel's toys and merchandise brought him fabulous fame and money. Marvin Glass & Associates collected royalties on all the Evel products, and for several years we all rode Evel Knievel products to the pot of gold at the end of the rainbow.

Between 1973 and 1978, Evel earned about $5 million in royalties from our products. Unfortunately, he believed that his royalty income would never end. He bought boats, yachts, numerous mink coats, fancy cars, and several homes. The Evel Knievel Stunt Cycle was his single largest source of income, and sales were beginning to wane after five years. Evel refused to believe that his money was running out, so in January 1978 I decided to fly down to Ft. Lauderdale, Florida, to try to make him understand reality.

Evel's house in Ft. Lauderdale was modest, but he had bought it because it included a long pier on Florida's Intracoastal Waterway. That's where he docked his yacht, a 120-foot Dutch-built Feadship—the Rolls Royce of private yachts. Evel lived on the extravagant yacht, not in the house.

When I walked onto the dock, I was a little nervous about being the bearer of bad news. I saw a sleek Riva racing boat tied up behind his yacht. I didn't know anything about Italian racing boats, but it looked spectacular. Evel asked me to go for a ride on it and I thought, "Why not have some fun before breaking the bad news?" When he turned the key and started the engines, I heard the sound of awesome, brute power. It sounded like three lions roaring right in my ear. I was already scared and we were still tied to the dock.

As we pulled away, I saw that the speed limit sign said twenty-five miles per hour and no wake. Evel pushed the throttles forward and was immediately going sixty, with giant rooster tails of water rising behind us and waves crashing on the sides of the channel. That speed in a boat is ridiculous; the faster a boat goes, the more it bounces and bucks on the water. Evel asked me if I wanted more, but I said no. He just wanted to scare me and show me how fast his boat could go—that was his real toy. The ride wasn't over soon enough for me.

That night we had dinner in a fabulous dining room on his yacht. I had a beer, but Evel was a serious drinker and rambled on and on drunkenly. I decided to wait until the morning to tell him the bad news. When I told him his income was declining, he didn't believe me. He was in complete denial and said the toy would keep selling. We had a friendly goodbye and that was the last time I saw him.

Evel was a tragic character. Every time his body healed, he busted it up again. When he had millions and millions of dollars, he spent it all. About a year after I went to see Evel in Florida, two Internal Revenue Service agents showed up at Marvin Glass and ordered us to send any future checks for Evel to the IRS. Evel was uncontrollable and often got himself into trouble.

In 1977, Evel was convicted in California of beating his former press agent with a baseball bat and sentenced to six months in jail. The conviction had a devastating effect on sales of his toys. That's the downside of a real celebrity. A fantasy figure, like Spiderman, Batman, or Wonder Woman, always behaves. Superman never got arrested for beating someone up. Batman never went to jail. The kids didn't know anything about Evel's bad behavior, but the adults knew, and they were the ones who paid for the toys.

Chapter 12

Marvin Exits the Stage

arvin Glass was a love-him-or-hate-him kind of guy. He was an irrepressible, hyperactive genius who lived on the edge of his emotions. Years after he died, I looked up the definitions for manic-depressive, paranoid, and schizophrenic, and he seemed to be all of these things. But I wasn't a qualified judge of these conditions—I just knew that despite his remarkable eccentricities, I loved him.

Marvin was articulate, passionate, and playful. He never slept more than five hours a night. He was a serious reader and had a photographic memory, devouring three or four books a week. Marvin studied philosophy, history, psychology, religion, and biographies—he never read fiction. Aside from creating toys, his major entertainment was debating these subjects while sitting in his living room or at his dining room table. He spoke in a raspy, low voice because he smoked two or three packs of unfiltered English Ovals cigarettes a day.

If the conversation drifted to sports, movies, or television, Marvin quickly changed it back to the subjects he loved. When I was first getting to know Marvin, I decided to test his knowledge. Marvin's favorite philosopher was Friedrich Nietzsche, and I bought a copy of *Beyond Good and Evil*. I tried to read it, but it was way over my head and I didn't get very far. I did write down one of Nietzsche's key phrases, however, which had to do with the "historical beginnings of artistic creation."

I was sitting with Marvin around his dinner table one evening when I mentioned Nietzsche's key phrase. It was like winding up a toy and setting it in motion. Marvin started an intense discussion about Nietzsche and the contrasting writing styles of Sophocles and other Greek playwrights. Marvin could bullshit as well as anyone, but he was brilliant on the topics he studied, including Carl Jung, who founded analytical psychology. It was at that dinner that Marvin told me he had been in psychoanalysis for many years.

In addition to being a great reader, Marvin was a serious art collector. He knew that I also loved art and one day called me in to show me a beautiful bronze sculpture of a medieval knight. It was only about eight inches tall. Marvin had just bought the knight and told me about the Russian artist Eugene Dobos. When Dobos was eleven years old, he was playing with a live grenade that exploded. The grenade blew off eight of his fingers and blinded him in one eye. As a young artist with artificial metal pincer hands, Dobos was nevertheless able to weld and create beautiful sculptures.

Marvin had bought a few of Dobos's pieces and asked what I thought of the knight. I replied, "I loved it the instant I saw it. There's something unique about the technique that makes it look unlike other steel sculptures. It looks cute and funny, almost like plush." Handing me the sculpture, he said, "It's yours." I tried to say no but he insisted. The gorgeous knight was the first serious piece of art that I owned and I still have it on display. He continued to buy me small gifts of expensive sculptures, despite my protestations.

Marvin always lived above his means. He bought a lot of artwork and spent a fortune on his Evanston home. When he made more money, he spent it. Marvin owned 75 percent of MGA in 1972, according to a *Wall Street Journal* article. That year we grossed $8.7 million on products that were responsible for $175 million in retail sales, according to the same article. Marvin controlled the business, but he gave all of his partners a piece of the action so we wouldn't leave. He was a generous and spontaneous boss. I never had to ask him for a raise.

When my first son, Marc, was born on June 11, 1969, we were living in our second apartment on the North Side of Chicago. When Marlene was expecting again, we decided to move to Highland Park, a lovely suburb north of Chicago where many of our married college friends lived. It was winter of 1972 and my salary at Marvin Glass had increased from $10,000 to $25,000. When I started my first job at American Hospital Supply for $5,200 a year, I remember thinking that if I ever made $25,000 a year it would be a dream come true.

We found a new house in a terrific neighborhood and considered purchasing it. It was a two-story Georgian with four bedrooms, three and a half baths, and a full basement. It was perfect, but it was a little more than I wanted to pay. My brother Gene had just bought a new home in Morton Grove, Illinois, and I was thinking of paying three times more than what he had paid for his house. I was sure that my dad would give me a lecture if I told him I was thinking of spending that much money.

After talking to Marvin about the house, he told me to buy it and said, "It sounds like a steal." I didn't know how Marvin's mind worked at that time, but later on I learned that he had thought to himself, *If Jeffrey buys that home, he'll work harder.* That's what Marvin did himself. I bought that wonderful house and worked harder and made more money and had more fun. My dad was proud of my success in my budding career. He loved my new house, and when I told him the price, he didn't utter a word.

Marvin taught me a lot about the toy business in the seven years I worked for him. He also taught me what I wouldn't want to do if I ever ran the company, which I couldn't imagine doing at that point. I wanted to enjoy my personal life as well as work. I wanted to travel and see the world. On May 7, 1972, Marlene and I welcomed our second son, Michael, into the world. I loved being the father of two young boys and I wanted to spend lots of time with my family. I was the opposite of Marvin.

Marvin didn't allow children in the studio. He adamantly opposed testing any of our toys or games with children. He was afraid they couldn't keep quiet about whatever new toy they played with at the studio. Marvin thought we had enough young parents with children working for the company. We couldn't even take any of our prototypes home to try out with our own kids and families. At night everything got locked in the vault.

One day we had a new client in for a presentation. During the meeting, he asked Marvin if he ever tested prototypes with kids. Marvin looked the client straight in the eye and said, "I haven't seen a kid in twenty years." We all roared with laughter, but Marvin was serious.

Marvin worked hard and celebrated hard. It was easy to celebrate hard in Chicago. Mister Kelly's was a famous Chicago nightclub on North Rush Street that operated from 1953 to 1975. Among the notables who performed there were Barbra Streisand, Lenny Bruce, Dick Gregory, Bob Newhart, and Ella Fitzgerald. Mister Kelly's had a tiny stage, and audience members felt like they were sitting in someone's living room. There was also a slightly elevated bar where you could sit and nurse one drink and see up-and-coming stars. In 1963, I had used a fake ID to get in and see a twenty-one-year-old Barbra Streisand belt out lots of show tunes, including "Cry Me a River" and "Happy Days Are Here Again."

Ten years later, on June 14, 1973, I celebrated Marvin's fifty-ninth birthday with him and ten other people at Mister Kelly's. I had just turned thirty years old and it was just three months since we had signed a contract with Evel Knievel. Marvin chose Mister Kelly's because he was a huge fan of a rising twenty-eight-year-old singer, Bette Midler. She was performing with Barry Manilow, her musical arranger and piano player. Bette had an enormous gay following and started her career singing at the Continental Baths, a gay bathhouse in New York City, which earned her the nickname Bathhouse Betty.

That night Bette sang many songs from her debut album, *The Divine Miss M*. The highlights were "Do You Want to Dance?" "Friends," and "Boogie Woogie Bugle Boy." Bette was her outrageous self, and the audience's enthusiasm and adulation made her show absolutely spectacular. I still smile when I remember what a fantastic time Marvin enjoyed while listening to Bette and Barry on his birthday.

Three weeks later, on July 8, 1973, Marvin suffered a massive stroke that paralyzed his left side. Eventually, he could walk with a limp and cane, but his left arm hung down, almost useless. His speech was slurred and the left side of his face drooped. I visited him a few days later in Highland Park Hospital. I was shocked to see this vibrant, wild, and crazy guy almost immobilized. We cried while I held his good hand, and Marvin told me he was glad to be alive. He promised he was going to change. "I'm going to give up smoking, coffee, stop working so hard and chasing women." As he lay there in his hospital bed, he pledged he was going to take vacations, sit by his pool, and relax and enjoy life. He lied.

Before his stroke, Marvin had bought a beautiful home in Miami for his fifth wife, Abby Rios, whom he had married in 1972 when he was fifty-seven years old. Abby was a beautiful thirty-four-year-old dancer. She moved to Miami with the understanding that Marvin would spend more time in Florida and not work so hard. Abby, who was from Puerto Rico, never got used to Chicago winters. After Abby moved, Marvin hired his latest girlfriend, Carol, to be a receptionist at the studio. Carol knew about Abby, but Abby didn't know about Carol, who was twenty years old, Chinese, and had been Marvin's mistress since 1971.

After Marvin's stroke, when he was still in the hospital, a friend arranged for Marvin to have a double room so Carol could sleep in the bed next to him. I wasn't there, but I heard about the fireworks when Abby came up from Miami to visit Marvin and found Carol living in his hospital room.

A few months later, he tried to get back to his old self, the energetic, chain-smoking Marvin. He had an elevator built at the office so he could get to the second floor. He tried to get back to work, but he could no longer communicate effectively—he couldn't pitch ideas to clients, fire up the creativity in his partners and designers, or terrorize employees who feared him. He couldn't romance women, yell through the studio speaker system, or argue politics, religion, or philosophy. Everything that made Marvin such a remarkable, original man was gone.

Marvin served as a fantastic mentor and father figure to me for six years and three months. He hired me as an unknown twenty-four-year-old and taught me everything about designing hit toys. He showed me how to build client relationships and make a profit in our highly competitive business. I owe him for everything I achieved in my career. But his horrible stroke had virtually incapacitated him and left him terribly frail. At fifty-nine, Marvin knew he was dying.

Marvin, however, being the fabulous showman he was, enjoyed one last great scene. While on his deathbed, his wife Abby and girlfriend Carol had a titanic fight in front of him. My good friend Rouben Terzian, a partner and toy designer, witnessed the confrontation. Marvin asked Rouben to come to his bedroom about an hour before he died. In Bill Paxton's wonderful book, *A World Without Reality: Inside Marvin Glass's Toy Vault!*, Rouben recalled, "So I go up there and there is Marvin reclined in his bed. Carol Scott on one side, Abby on the other side. Carol is his mistress. Abby was his wife. The two of them are fighting and calling each other names like 'You bitch!' and 'You would be on the street if it wasn't for Marvin!' and 'What corner did he find you?' Marvin turned to me and gestured with his finger for me to come closer. He whispered while struggling to speak, 'Rouben, these women are killing me.' And then he slowly looks up at me and smiles on the side of his mouth. He couldn't wink. But he tried very hard to wink even though he was so weak. He was in heaven that they were fighting over him. One hour later he died."

Marvin died on January 7, 1974, six months after his stroke. Marvin's funeral was exactly as he would have wanted it. The first three rows were filled with sobbing women.

Abby, his fifth wife, looked sexy and beautiful as always. Elizabeth, Marvin's former longtime live-in girlfriend, was there. There were so many other grieving women that I was confused about who they all were. Marvin loved chaos almost as much as he loved women.

Marvin's two daughters and his step-daughter were there. Diana was his daughter with Dorothy, who was both his first and third wife. Linda, his stepdaughter, was Dorothy's daughter from her first marriage. Marvin also had a daughter, Denise, who lived with her mother somewhere in Texas. Marvin had supported Denise her whole life. She was around twenty years old and Marvin had talked to her on the phone every Sunday. Her physical resemblance to Marvin was uncanny.

Many toy industry kingpins attended Marvin's funeral, including Lionel Weintraub, his friend and the president of Ideal Toy Company; Mattel founders Ruth and Elliot Handler; and Hasbro's CEO, Merrill Hassenfeld. Evel Knievel served as a pallbearer. All of the sixty or so employees from the studio were there. Marvin, who always loved to be the center of attention, would have been thrilled with the crowd.

When we opened the studio a week after Marvin died, none of us were prepared for his absence. We all had known he was dying, but we were still shocked when it happened. Marvin was always at the office, or we were at his home for meetings, almost until the end. I never remember him taking a vacation in all the years I worked for him. He abhorred vacations and hated when his employees took them. Marvin also hated three-day national holiday weekends, Memorial Day, Labor Day, and the Fourth of July. If the Fourth fell on a Saturday, we didn't have to work. If it fell on a Sunday, we had to work Monday. We only got the Thursday of Thanksgiving weekend off, never the Friday or Saturday. We worked every Saturday but got off early, at around 3:00 p.m. We all worked that hard because Marvin worked that hard.

We carried on and the business prospered. But I missed Marvin terribly, both for the wonderful things we did together and for his dynamic personality. I missed the endless dinner parties at his home and the cooking of his chef, Poy Tom; flying first class to five New York Toy Fairs with him; and flying to L.A. and meeting Mattel founders Ruth and Elliot Handler. I also missed his craziness, energy, and passion; his screaming about politics and religion; his pretending to be a tyrant, but in truth being a softie with a generous heart; and his excitement at seeing a new toy prototype. Most of all, I just missed my friend Marvin! He was one of a kind, and I'm thankful he was my mentor for almost seven years.

In 2011, I read Walter Isaacson's fabulous biography of Steve Jobs. As I began reading, all I could think was that Steve Jobs and Marvin Glass were cast from the same mold. They were both visionaries and creative marketing geniuses. That was their exceptional talent. Jobs couldn't write a line of complex code and wasn't a designer. Marvin couldn't build a prototype or sketch a toy.

They both only accepted excellence. If a product or concept was an A-minus or a B-plus, it was "shit." Perfection was their standard, and anything less was unacceptable. They could be brutal to work for. Employees loved them or hated them, often on the same day. Being neutral about them was impossible. Their personal lives were a mess. Work was the only meaning to their lives. But Steve and Marvin were both fantastical characters who touched people the world over.

The biggest differences between the two men were the industries they worked in and the times they lived in. Steve Jobs was a rock star inventor, who worked at what became one of the largest industries in the world, at the dawning of the computer business. Jobs became world-famous by using the internet, television, and social media to publicize and promote himself and his products. Jobs's death in 2011 was mourned by millions of people around the globe.

Marvin's toys and games brought fun, entertainment, and joy to hundreds of millions of children and families around the world by the time he died in 1974, thirty-seven years before Jobs. Marvin, however, received only a tiny fraction of Jobs's fame. Only a small group of toy executives, employees, friends, and family shared Marvin's extraordinary life. So few knew of him at all. He's still with me every day. Without Marvin, my story couldn't be written.

Chapter 13

Movies and TV: The *Jaws* Game and the Mickey Mouse Phone

We continued designing toys and games, but the business was different without Marvin's dazzling showmanship and personality. Marvin had brought a former colleague from New York, Anson Isaacson, into the company as a partner in 1971. Marvin and Anson had worked together in the early 1960s, when Anson was at Ideal Toy. We were all aware that Marvin was grooming Anson to take over the company as managing partner, but there was still some surprise and mild resentment by senior partners when Marvin made it official—so many good people had worked at Glass for decades. Anson now ran the ship and occupied Marvin's beautiful, spacious office with the gorgeous art, furniture, and 500-gallon saltwater aquarium.

Anson ran the company, but he couldn't replace Marvin—no one could. Anson was in his mid-fifties and a well-respected businessman in the industry. Under his command we continued to be profitable. But unlike Marvin, who had loved to spend hours in the model shop talking with all the employees and having fun playing with all the prototypes, Anson remained upstairs in his office, ruling from above. He was a tough manager who focused on making money. Anson, a stocky man with short, dark hair and glasses, was married with two children. At heart, he was a businessman who ran a toy company, not a toy inventor who ran a business.

Early on, Anson wanted us to diversify outside of the toy business. Most of the partners opposed his idea, including me, but we did it anyway. MGA went on to design projects that Marvin never would have approved. We tried to create hardware products for Black & Decker. We made sample houseware items for Amway and Tupperware. Thankfully, the consumer product companies never took us seriously and we soon gave it up. We went back to where we belonged, which was focusing on toys and games. One change that Anson made, however, remained— MGA went back to designing toy guns.

Marvin Glass & Associates had made millions of dollars by licensing Evel Knievel products, and Anson decided to expand our licensing business. He hired a new partner, Joe Callan, a Chicago native who specialized in licensing products and knew advertising people. Joe had a new wife and kids from a previous marriage. He was a dark-haired man in his early fifties who loved to drive his Rolls-Royce. He was a fun-loving, gregarious guy, and the two of us took four trips together. We traveled to Las Vegas, Reno, Palm Springs, and Los Angeles, trying to make a deal with Frank Sinatra.

We were chasing Sinatra, trying to get his approval for us to license a fragrance called *Sinatra*, as well as a new suit with an elegant lining depicting Frank wearing his trademark hat. If we succeeded, we had both a fragrance company and a clothing company lined up and ready to go. Joe and I met several of Sinatra's managers and finally got to his last handler—Mickey Rudin, Frank's attorney. If Rudin liked the deal, we hoped we'd get to meet Sinatra and pitch it to him ourselves. We set up a beautiful presentation for Rudin. He walked in, looked at our meticulously prepared display, said, "Frank doesn't need this shit," and walked out. Deal over. But what fun it was to try!

As far as I was concerned, MGA needed to change its culture. Half our customers were little girls, and hiring more women designers just made sense. It was time to help break the "Glass" ceiling and improve the gender ratio at our studio. We had only one female toy designer at the time, Alison Katzman. She was a neighbor of one of our partners, Burt Meyer, and a wonderful sculptor and artist. Burt had seen Alison's work and suggested that she come work for Glass, which she did in 1970. Alison created many successful products and is best known for designing the Blythe doll, which came out in 1972.

I got my chance to hire a woman to be a toy designer not long after Marvin died, in the fall of 1974, when I interviewed one of the most wonderful, creative women I've ever known. When Kathy Dunn walked in for her interview, I was entranced. Kathy sparkled. She was a stunning blonde with laughing blue eyes and a lovely smile who wore her hair in a pixie cut. Kathy, tall and athletic, was in her early thirties and divorced with no children.

Kathy's design portfolio was excellent, with some good toy and doll concepts. I immediately offered her a job as a toy designer. I didn't bother to confer with any other partners. I knew they would agree, and they did. Kathy Dunn turned out to be an excellent designer and created several profitable products, including the wonderful Tiffany Taylor and Tuesday Taylor dolls in 1974. The ads for Tuesday Taylor dolls ran, "Tuesday's world is full of magic," and they sold well for several years.

In 1975, the movie *Jaws* was released and I was blown away when I saw it. I loved the deep, pulsing music and how you were afraid before you even saw the shark. I thought the actual *Jaws* puppet that they built for filming was fantastic. I think that nowadays, with computer animation, something wonderful is lost in movies that don't use actual puppets. But I loved the movie so much it inspired me to design the toy shark and create the Jaws game.

Again, it was Lionel Weintraub at Ideal who recognized the game's value and snapped it up. The original box reads, *The Game of JAWS*, with the word "Jaws" in bright red letters. The box displays an enormous, frightening shark with its open mouth bristling with giant teeth. The caption reads, "It's you against the great white shark. One wrong move... and the *Jaws* go snap!" The movie went through three sequels and the game sold well for many years. It's still sold today as The Game of Jaws. A Game of Strategy and Suspense!

Howard Morrison, my business partner and dear friend, dreamed up another hugely profitable product in 1976—the Mickey Mouse telephone. Howard said that the Bell telephone company was looking for a unique edge to help them sell phones. With his wonderful sense of humor, Howard got the idea of making a phone out of a famous animated character and picked the perfect one: Mickey Mouse.

Howard had Mike Ferris, one of our sculptors, create a fabulous model of a smiling, eighteen-inch-tall Mickey standing with his right arm up on a square wooden base. Mickey wore shiny red shorts and bright yellow shoes and held a bright yellow phone in his right hand. You lifted the handset out of Mickey's hand when you wanted to talk, and hung it up by placing the phone back on Mickey's hand. Our prototype worked because we took all the guts out of a real Western Electric phone to build our Mickey Mouse phone. We plugged it in and it functioned perfectly.

Happily, we got the rights from the Walt Disney Company to use Mickey Mouse. The Disney people were skeptical of our idea (as were we, for that matter), but they agreed that we could make phones in Mickey's image if we could make a deal with a telephone manufacturer. We arranged to pitch our Mickey Mouse phone to executives at Western Electric, but when we did, the reaction we got was a disaster. The drift of the conversation went something like this: "Are you fricking kidding? That's a toy product with a juvenile preschool character. We make real phones and serious products. You took our guts to make your toy work. Get lost!" They didn't see the fun and humor that came with Mickey handing you the phone when a call came in. As often happens, however, many successful ideas zig when everyone else is zagging.

There was another company that was manufacturing inexpensive telephones, American Telecommunications Corporation in El Monte, California. We pitched the idea to them and they agreed with us and zigged. They understood the concept and the humor and quickly bought it. They turned the Mickey Mouse phone into a blockbuster, first with a rotary dial, then with a push-button dial.

The huge mistake we made is that we didn't immediately go after all of the other popular characters out there for phones. MGA didn't grab Snoopy, Bugs Bunny, or Winnie the Pooh when we had the chance. We later made a giant red lips phone and a Pac-Man phone, but nothing approached the triumph we had with Mickey Mouse. We missed our chance to dominate the market for adorable telephones. Howard Morrison and I still own Mickey Mouse phones. Howard created this wonderful product that brought joy to so many in the 1970s and started a new trend in telephones.

The lesson we all learned is to do the unexpected. It became one of the great secrets of our success in the toy business. The hard part is that you just have to do it. You also can't take no for an answer. Just because one client turns down a product doesn't mean it's not a great idea. The experts are not always the ones to make a new and gutsy product. Persistence is essential, especially if the idea is unusual and cutting edge.

An excellent example of persistence is 1982's Cabbage Patch Kids, which were one of the first Christmas items that inspired desperate parents to get into vicious fistfights in toy stores. The Cabbage Patch Kids were cuter and less obese versions of the Little People fabric dolls created by Xavier Roberts, a twenty-one-year-old art student at Truett McConnell Junior College in Georgia. To his credit, Xavier zigged. I wish we had.

In 1982, the major doll makers were Mattel and Ideal Toy Company. They had multiple lines of baby dolls and Barbie dolls and were considered the industry experts. Both companies turned down the Cabbage Patch Kids. Eventually, Coleco agreed to manufacture the Cabbage Patch dolls, even though they'd never made a doll before. Each doll had to be unique, which is difficult to do in manufacturing, but Coleco figured it out. The marketing for the dolls was unique and ingenious. Children "adopted" a doll—they didn't buy it—and it came with a birth certificate to "prove" it.

When the line debuted in 1982, children around the world flipped for the soft, floppy dolls. A phenomenon known as "the Cabbage Patch Kid Riots" ensued. Security guards armed with baseball bats protected the stock, store employees threw new doll boxes into masses of screaming buyers, and parents drove hundreds of miles to find a doll for Christmas morning. The brand of Cabbage Patch Kids and accessories went on to earn more than $2 billion. Nice zig, Xavier Roberts. Nice zig, Coleco.

A decade earlier, however, in the early 1970s, other trends were emerging in the toy industry. Electronic toys and games were just becoming the rage. MGA needed to add an electrical engineer to our staff, and in 1972 Howard Morrison hired a man he had worked with earlier at Strombecker's Toys, Al Keller. Keller worked on projects with batteries, switches, and electrical components. Keller was a big man who stood six-four, but he was reserved and unobtrusive.

Al Keller was our only electrical engineer and had recently received a raise. His job was not in jeopardy; he was a good and necessary employee. Keller had just returned from New York, where he and another model maker had delivered a game to Ideal Toy called Tin Can Alley, a rifle shooting game. Ideal loved Tin Can Alley, bought it from us, and made a lot of money on it.

Al Keller and I worked on different types of products, and I only spoke to him in the hallways to say hi. I was vaguely aware that he was married with a young daughter and lived in a house on the Southwest Side of Chicago. As far as I could tell, Keller seemed like a normal, quiet guy, right up until he pulled out a gun and shot six people on a beautiful summer's day in Chicago in 1976.

Chapter 14

Tragedy

Most mornings at around 9:00 a.m., the ten partners gathered for a meeting in Anson's office, which had formerly been Marvin's. To me, the office was still Marvin's. Marvin had chosen the art, plush leather furniture, rosewood paneling, antique light fixtures, and lamps. On the parquet walnut floor was an expensive silk oriental rug. Marvin also had picked out the 500-gallon fish tank built into the wall. It was a live marine painting with gorgeous saltwater specimens, including two miniature, six-inch-long sharks. The vast, impeccable office could have been on the cover of *Architectural Digest* magazine.

All ten partners normally attended our morning meeting, which Anson announced over the studio intercom. For the next hour or so, the partners discussed projects, clients, employees, and whatever else came up. On the morning of July 27, I stopped briefly by Kathy's office on my way into the meeting, as was my habit, but couldn't chat long because I was already late. Kathy's workspace was along the corridor on the way to Anson's office.

That day, a Tuesday, our meeting broke up a little earlier than normal, right before 10:00 a.m. All the partners left Anson's office except Anson, Joe Callan, and me. Anson was sitting at his desk and Joe and I were sitting on the long leather couch along the wall to his left.

At 9:55 a.m., the phone next to me rang and I answered it. It was Pauline, our receptionist, telling me that Jim Salem was calling back to talk to me. I paused and Pauline sensed that the name didn't register with me. She jumped in with, "The guy from Alabama who chatted with you about Evel Knievel." I remembered that Jim and I had talked a week earlier. Jim, a professor of American studies at the University of Alabama, had asked if he could call me if he needed more information. There wasn't any more I could say about Evel, but I liked Jim and replied, "Of course."

I told Pauline to put the call through to an office across the hall that belonged to Jim Coffee, our in-house patent attorney, who wasn't at work that day. Coffee's office was always immaculate, and he never minded when the partners used his room. I walked out the back door of Anson's office, which was made of solid wood, and closed it behind me. I stepped into Coffee's room, which was about ten feet to the right and across the hall from Anson's office.

Al Keller arrived and parked his car just as I was taking Pauline's call about Jim Salem. Keller entered the studio and walked up the back stairs that led to the toy designer's area. He was carrying two guns, a 9 mm semiautomatic pistol and a .25-caliber revolver. The guns may have been concealed in his jacket pockets, or he might have been carrying them in his hands, but no one noticed them. No one would have paid attention to an experienced employee coming in late for work. Al was quiet and typically didn't chat with others anyway. He headed first to the partners meeting in Anson's office.

Keller advanced through two heavy hallway doors that stood between the toy designer's area in the back of the building and Anson's office in the front. When Keller opened Anson's back door, he would have expected to see most of the partners in the room. Instead, there were only Anson sitting at his desk five feet away and Joe on the sofa where I left them moments before. Anson always turned toward the door when it opened;

perhaps he was looking to see if I was returning. The first two shots I heard while sitting in Jim Coffee's office were fired point-blank from the 9 mm pistol into Anson's face; he died instantly. The next three shots pierced Joe's chest.

When I heard the five shots, I didn't believe the gunfire was from a real gun. I thought it was noise from a cap gun or some other product—as toy inventors, we knew that great sound was often crucial to a product's design. Why would there be gunfire in this ultra-secure toy studio? I didn't hide. I calmly said to Jim Salem, "Hold on a second; I'll be right back." I put the call on hold and went to check out the noise. Keller must have walked out of Anson's office and toward the toy designers' area just as I was putting the call on hold and getting up out of the chair to go see what happened.

When I stepped into the hall, I saw that the back door was wide open. I knew I had closed it on my way out. I walked in and saw Anson slumped back in his chair. The sight was so horrible I thought it couldn't be real. Then it hit me that I had heard actual gunshots. My eyes registered what I saw, but my brain refused to believe it. The battle between my vision and brain continued until I turned and saw Joe on the sofa, blood staining his shirt. Joe dropped to his knees, looked at me, and without a word fell face-forward onto the floor.

It never entered my mind that the shooter was an employee. I assumed the killer had come in the front entrance. It didn't register with me that the back door was wide open and the front door of the office was still closed. I ran out the front door of Anson's office toward Pauline in the reception area screaming, "Where did he go?" Pauline looked at me like I was crazy. She hadn't heard the shots through the closed front door of Anson's office. Her area was thirty feet away and partially blocked from Anson's office by the new elevator that had been installed for Marvin after his stroke.

At that moment, someone ran out a side door and into the reception area screaming for Pauline to call the police and an ambulance. That side door led to the back of the building where the toy designers worked, and that's when I realized the carnage was still going on. Instinctively, I knew something terrible had happened to Kathy. The employees near Kathy's office would have had no warning. They wouldn't have been able to hear the gunshots from Anson's office because of the two heavy hallway doors.

I started shaking when it hit me that I must have missed seeing the killer and being shot to death by seconds. I realized, in that moment, that it was a miracle I never saw the killer and the killer never saw me. It was a miracle I was alive.

I was later told that after shooting Anson and Joe, Keller headed to the back of the building where the toy designers worked. The toy designers' corridor contained nine offices, four on one side and five on the other; these included Kathy Dunn and Alison Katzman's shared office. The end of the corridor dead-ended in a large office used by one of the partners. The offices had glass sliding doors that were all open on that morning.

When Keller turned into the toy designers' area, he first shot Don Nix, thirty-two, in the back. Don fell to the floor, still alive. Keller then fired twice at partner Burt Meyer. Incredibly, Burt wasn't hit, but a bullet went through the crease of his pants. Burt showed me the bullet hole in his trousers later that day.

Keller walked into the second office on the left, which was the space shared by Alison Katzman and Kathy Dunn. Alison was not in the office at that moment. Kathy was sitting at her desk and sketching at her drawing board when Keller shot her in the head. Kathy died instantly.

Keller stepped into the hallway and saw Doug Montague, thirty-four, his best friend at work. Doug's office was right across from his buddy Keller's, and Doug was outside his office and looking at Keller as he approached. Keller took time to reload his pistol before he shot Doug. Despite being shot three times—in the spleen, abdomen, and liver— Doug was still alive.

At the far end of the corridor, one of the toy designers, Jerry Pinsler, saw what happened next. Jerry said that after Keller shot Doug Montague, he stopped in the hallway, put the gun to his own throat, and squeezed the trigger. The bullet passed through Keller's throat and blew a hole through the top of Jerry's glass office door. Keller dropped the gun and fell to the floor, but he was still alive. He reached over, grabbed the weapon, struggled to his feet, put the gun to his temple and fired. (See diagram below.)

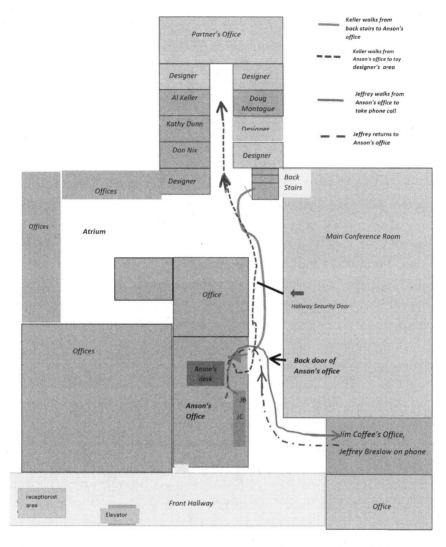

Marvin Glass & Associates, 2nd Floor, 818 N. LaSalle St, July 27, 1976.

Within minutes, the studio was swarming with police and para-medics. I couldn't bring myself to go to the toy designers' area after the carnage I had seen in Anson's office. I couldn't bear it. The paramedics treated the wounded before removing the bodies. Joe Callan was still breathing when they rushed him out, but I soon heard that he died before reaching the hospital. I learned that Kathy had been shot in the head and died instantly as she sketched at her drawing board—my worst fears had been confirmed. Don Nix and Doug Montague were both fighting for their lives in the hospital.

I returned to Jim Coffee's office and sat down at his desk, crying uncontrollably. My body shook and my grief was unimaginable. I got hold of myself and called my dad to tell him there had been a shooting at the office and some people had been killed and wounded. I said, "I'm OK, Dad, I wasn't hurt. Please call mom and tell her I'm OK." I called Marlene and told her the same. I didn't want her to hear the news from someone else and kept reassuring her I was OK. My son Marc had just turned seven and Michael was four. When I thought about them, I started to cry again because I was glad they still had a father. I was horrified that Anson's and Joe's children didn't.

While the bodies were being removed from the studio, homicide commander Joseph DiLeonardi saw me sitting in Jim Coffee's office and asked who I was. I told him I was a partner. He then handed me two pages of the notes that were in Keller's sock. Keller's scribblings were about the "conspiracy" of the fourteen employees at Glass who were out to kill him. Anson's was the first name on the list and mine was second. Some other partners' names were on the list too. Don Nix, Kathy Dunn, and Doug Montague's names were not on the list.

Keller also had written that the blacks and Mexicans were taking over Chicago and that his neighbor was after his wife. I felt an immediate, visceral reaction to these words. Feeling an overwhelming urge to destroy them, I showed the sheets of paper to no one and burned the paranoid ramblings in an ashtray. I don't know why the commander handed me those notes—perhaps it was because Keller was dead and there was no mystery to solve other than why anyone would commit such an unthinkable act.

As I sat in Jim Coffee's office, I realized that I had just been sitting in that same chair and talking on that same phone just a short time earlier.

I knew the caller, Jim Salem, wasn't still on hold. Jim had called me to talk business, but his telephone call saved my life.

When the police allowed it, we sent everyone home and closed the studio for the rest of the week. Flynn Barr and Joe Washington, our maintenance men, stayed behind to clean up the blood.

Chapter 15

Aftermath

T he police investigation into Al Keller moved quickly. Within a short time, the evidence showed that he had suffered from undiagnosed and untreated paranoid schizophrenia. Police interviews revealed that Keller had displayed classic symptoms, including delusions that grew more powerful and threatening over time. His behavior and language had deteriorated markedly in the weeks before the shooting.

Keller had always been quiet and mild-mannered in the office, but some employees reported that he changed into a different person when he was outside of work. He became combative and belligerent, particularly when he drank. Keller was also known to be fascinated with handguns and would sometimes bring real guns into the office. He would show them off to his coworkers, which made some of them uncomfortable, but it was always tolerated.

"To many people who knew big, friendly Al Keller, he was perhaps the last man in the world they would expect to go berserk," reported the *Chicago Tribune* the day after the shooting. "He was a good neighbor, a solid family man, and, after seven years at Glass, a valued, trusted employee whose work in designing electric toy parts was respected. But somewhere inside Al Keller a poisonous seed was growing."

The week before the shooting, model maker Frank Wimmer observed a heated altercation between Keller and partner Gordon Barlow. It was just a few days before a scheduled presentation to Ideal Toy executives of the electronic rifle shooting game Tin Can Alley. Wimmer recalled, "Al and Gordon had an argument about Tin Can Alley the week before the shooting. We were running out of time for a deadline on a meeting that day. Tin Can Alley was supposed to work for the meeting, but we couldn't get it to work right. Gordon kept checking up on us and... we were having trouble. Gordon Barlow was so mad at Keller. Just as I walked up...Gordon saw me coming, sort of piped down, and left. That's when I sat down with Al at his cubicle. He was all nervous and couldn't even concentrate. I asked Al, 'What's going on? What's the problem?' And Al just pulled open his desk drawer, he grabbed one gun, a real one, and sort of showed it to me, and I looked, and then there was another one in there too. And he grabbed one and he said, 'I ought to shoot that bastard.' Then he put the gun back in and closed the drawer."

Model maker Terry Webb described what happened later that afternoon during the Tin Can Alley presentation to Ideal Toy executives Lionel Weintraub and Julie Cooper. Anson Isaacson, Frank Wimmer, Al Keller, Terry Webb, and others were in the presentation room for MGA. After the toy had been shown to the Ideal executives, they were hesitant about whether to buy it. Suddenly, Isaacson turned on his employees and verbally criticized them and the toy gun. Anson told them to "get this fucking shit outta here!" according to Webb. The design team was devastated to be publicly criticized like that after all their hard work on the project. Wimmer, Webb, and Keller talked afterward and called Anson "an asshole." More tellingly, Keller stated, "That motherfucker needs a bullet in his head!" Ironically, Lionel Weintraub and Ideal later bought the Tin Can Alley shooting game and introduced it in 1977. Tin Can Alley was a hit.

At the end of that contentious workday, partner Howard Morrison was getting ready to leave when Al Keller walked in. Unfortunately, Morrison had to be at an office roller-skating party and could only talk with Keller for a short time. Morrison later told the police that Keller had been complaining that MGA didn't appreciate his work and that some coworkers seemed to be conspiring against him, according to a *Chicago Tribune* article. Morrison thought he had convinced Keller that both he and his work were valued by the firm before he left for the evening. Chillingly, on the day of the shootings, Keller left one bullet on the chair in Howard's office. No one will ever know if Keller left the bullet intentionally or not.

On the evening after the presentation to the Ideal executives, Keller sat outside at a picnic table with his neighbor and friend John Stefanich, a Chicago police officer. They would often go shooting together. According to Stefanich, Keller was behaving oddly that night. Keller wouldn't sit in their normal place on the back porch and told Stefanich it was because, "I better not sit over there. Someone's trying to kill me." They talked and joked for a couple of hours over beers, then Keller suddenly stood up about midnight and said, "Somebody's out to get me. You guys might be in the way. I just want you to know that." Stefanich told Keller to sit down and relax because no one was out to get him, but Keller wouldn't listen. Stefanich recalled, "I couldn't believe it. He didn't have an enemy in the world that I knew of. Everyone liked him."

The morning of the shooting, Keller's wife, Joan, saw him preparing to take a pistol to work and asked him why. "Someone at work is trying to kill me. But everything will be OK," reported the *Chicago Sun-Times*. Joan was concerned and phoned one of our receptionists after he left the house. "Al is on the way to the shop, and he's bringing a couple of guns." The receptionist, Maureen McGowan, told Sam Cottone, an experienced model maker, about the call.

"When I heard that Al's wife called to say he was bringing a gun, I didn't figure that Al was going up there to shoot anybody," Cottone told the *Sun-Times*. "A lot of times, he was just planning to go shooting with John Stefanich. One time Al brought in a gun, but I knew he was going shooting and needed a repair. I made a little pin for it. I thought he had a couple more guns that needed to be fixed or something like that." Shortly after Keller's wife phoned the office, the shooting began.

Anson Isaacson had worked at MGA for five years, but he rarely interacted with Keller. Anson must have known who he was, but I doubt they ever talked directly. When Keller opened the back door to Anson's office, I'm sure it was the first time Keller had been in that room. Joe Callan also never interacted with Keller. I doubt they'd ever said more than hello to each other in the hallway.

Kathy Dunn is gone and I'm still here. Decades have passed. She is still only thirty-two years old and hasn't aged a day. We were the same age, and when I celebrate family milestones, I think of Kathy and know that she should be enjoying her own family milestones. She should have lots of grandchildren and still be drawing beautiful pictures. I have displayed on my wall at home a framed sketch of one of the hundreds of toy ideas she drew. Next to it I have a photo of her, which I still cherish.

Don Nix was a young, married toy designer with a ten-year-old son. Keller's gunshot severed Don's spinal cord, and he never walked or rode his beloved bicycle again. He spent two months in a rehabilitation hospital, where I visited him several times. It was brutal to see him in that setting, but he eventually returned to work in a wheelchair. He worked with us for the next twelve years. Seeing him was a daily reminder of the shootings. We never escaped from them—never.

Doug Montague recovered from being shot three times. One day after the shooting, Doug told me that he initially thought Keller was firing rubber bullets, because it didn't hurt a lot at first. Doug said he screamed at Keller to get him to stop shooting him before he realized the bullets were real. After his injuries healed, Doug returned to MGA to continue his brilliant career as a toy designer. He designed the exterior case and stylish look of the Simon game that we licensed to Milton Bradley. Simon was a blockbuster, and thanks to Doug's incredible talent, it looked spectacular.

As I told the police after the shootings happened, "Nobody, nobody knew the extent of [Al Keller's] illness. There was no way to anticipate what happened." In the notes tucked in his socks, Keller had written on one page, "Paranoia? No. Now you will know why I am doing this." On another sheet he had written, "This is my revenge. God will take care of the rest." As an aside, the Chicago Police Department's official file on the Marvin Glass shootings was stolen, according to Bill Paxton in *Inside Marvin Glass's Toy Vault!*

The shootings happened on Tuesday, July 27, 1976. From the time everyone left the studio that Tuesday afternoon, we didn't see each other that week except briefly at the funerals. It was like we were all on a ship that had just sank but we were each in our own life rafts and just barely hanging on.

We had four funerals the rest of that week, two in one day. I was shocked to hear how many employees attended Keller's funeral. People who went said that it wasn't the Al they knew who did the shooting. Instead, it was someone else in his body. I did not go to Keller's funeral.

It was at those funerals that my future and the future of MGA were decided. It was then that the eight remaining partners briefly discussed who should be the new managing partner. We had seventy employees and needed a new leader for our thriving business. The logical person to take over was Harry Disko, who was the oldest partner and had been with MGA the longest. Harry, however, didn't want the job.

No one wanted the job, except for the one partner we could never accept, Gordon Barlow. He was a fabulous toy designer and inventor, but Gordon was an emotional roller coaster with a short temper and frequent mood swings. He frightened many people, including me. Gordon openly lobbied to be named managing partner, trying to convince the other partners that he was the logical person to lead the company. The other partners pulled me aside to tell me they would approve anyone *except* Gordon.

At thirty-three, I was by far the youngest of the eight partners. I wasn't ready for the job and didn't want it. But by the end of the week, all the partners, other than Gordon, told me they would vote for me. I realized I had no choice and accepted the position of managing partner.

I called Gordon on Saturday morning and went to his house to break the bad news. He was furious. He cursed and screamed, arguing that I was too young and he had been at Glass far longer than I had. That was true, but it was also beside the point. Gordon left MGA. After I left his house that morning, I never saw him again.

I had one more awful task ahead of me. As the new managing partner, I felt I needed to call Kathy Dunn's parents and express my condolences to them for the loss of their beloved daughter. Kathy was an only child. Her parents, grief-stricken, were gracious and kind during our brief call. My heart broke for them.

As the new managing partner, I would be in charge when we reopened the studio on Monday. I realized I had no idea what to say to my coworkers. Fortunately, a friend of mine found an experienced psychologist who specialized in working with survivors of group disasters and mass shootings. I called the psychologist on Sunday, and he agreed to come to the studio the next day. He explained that he would ask everyone to tell their story to the group, including where they were and how they survived that day. The best way to help people heal, he said, was by getting them to talk about the shooting.

I was scared to face the employees when we opened the studio on Monday morning. Even with the help of the psychologist, who ended up staying for a week, it was tough to get the office up and running again. It was hard to get people's minds back to designing toys. It was particularly difficult because we were in the business of making fun and happy products for children. The contrast between thinking about laughing and engaged children and the reality of the appalling bloodshed of Keller's murderous rampage was extreme.

I had to throw away Anson's chair and buy a new one before I moved into his office. I decided not to lock the back door that Keller had walked through to shoot Anson and Joe. I just had to get used to it, but it took more than a year before I stopped jumping up every time someone walked through that door.

I took a giant step as the new general manager and changed MGA's work culture within a few months of becoming the managing partner.

I didn't believe in working incredibly long hours. That idea had come from Marvin, who had no life outside of work. I decided that partners and employees should no longer have to work weekends or late nights. Everyone had a chance to enjoy a happy home life in addition to a happy work life. I think we ran more efficiently and were a happier and more productive office because of my decision. Happiness is important for a company that designs happy products. The employees loved it.

In the course of that year, I became good friends with Jim Salem, the professor who telephoned me on the morning of the shooting and saved my life. Now no longer with us, Jim spent forty-three years teaching at the University of Alabama in Tuscaloosa. His passions were Crimson Tide football, his four children, and home-cooked meals from Donna, his lovely wife. Jim wore wire-rimmed glasses, had a graying beard, and looked like a stereotypical college professor.

I called Jim the day after the shootings. When he answered, all I said was, "Thank you for saving my life," and started to sob. Three weeks later, I flew south and met Jim and his family and we became dear friends. Jim waited a year to tell me that he had made a recording of our telephone conversation on the morning of the shooting.

Unbeknownst to me, he was recording all of his interviews about Evel on a cassette tape recorder. He asked if I would like to have the cassette tape. I told him I was glad he hadn't disclosed that to me earlier, but now I'd be able to handle listening to it. The recording ran:

"Mr. Breslow, is it OK if I call you Jeff?'

"Sure."

"Oh Lordy. I know a lot about Evel. I think I need to talk with Anson; would that be possible?"

"Sure, I just left him in his office. I'll go and get him."

"Jeff, just one minute, I just have a few more questions for you, is that OK?"

"Sure."

We chatted for a moment until—*BANG! BANG!...BANG! BANG! BANG!*

I could hardly stand to listen. That morning was the first moment I felt mortal. Before the shooting, I always felt in control of my life and believed I could manage whatever happened to me. After the shooting, I understood I was not always in control, and no one else was either.

Many people said to me, "Thank God you were saved." But God didn't save me—a phone call saved me. I rationalized that if God had saved me, then He was responsible for the death of Kathy, Anson, Joe, and the wounding of Don and Doug. If God gets the credit for good, He must take the blame for bad. I lost my faith and belief in God that Tuesday morning.

Life became more precious, friends and family more cherished. I looked at my sons Marc and Michael with more love than I thought possible. As the years go by, my faith in people grows. Whenever possible, I make new, younger friends. I take responsibility for my life. I never drink and drive, nor do I text behind the wheel. I know that every day since *that* day is exceptional.

I will never recover from the senseless killings of Kathy, Anson, and Joe, or the heartbreaking trauma that we all endured. Now, every time I hear about another senseless shooting, my heart grows heavy and my eyes turn glassy. I understand the pain of those who by chance and luck escape to live another day. I was lucky to have friends and family to help me during the dreadful weeks and months that followed the rampage. Like survivors of a war, we buried our dead, healed our wounded, and rebuilt our lives.

For me personally, the tide turned that tragic year when I learned in the fall that Marlene was pregnant with our third child. I loved being the father of two little boys, Marc and Michael. My third child was and is a special gift for Marlene and me, although his birth almost became another tragedy.

When Joey was born on May 30, 1977, ten months after the shooting, he was two months premature. We didn't know if he would live. Joey weighed only two pounds when he was admitted to Evanston Hospital's Neonatal Intensive Care Unit (NICU). For weeks, no one knew if he would survive as he fought for his life in the NICU. Those agonizing weeks of uncertainty and fear remain etched in my memory.

Joey lived because of the total devotion of Dr. Thomas Gardner and the NICU nurses at Evanston Hospital. At one point, Dr. Gardner spent twenty-four hours straight next to Joey's tiny bed, ceaselessly caring for him and giving him every possible treatment. Marlene and I are eternally grateful to the neonatologist and the nurses for saving my son's life. Joey spent two months in the hospital. When we took him home, he weighed four and a half pounds. Today he is six-foot-one and 180 pounds, the biggest of my three wonderful sons.

Joey's birth and survival gave my life a brilliant spark at the end of that difficult year. However, Marvin Glass & Associates was still healing from the terrible aftereffects of Keller's rampage. We remained a viable company with a promising future, but the scuttlebutt in the toy industry was that MGA might not survive. Thanks to my gifted partner Howard Morrison, however, we were about to burst back into life and zoom into the toy industry stratosphere.

Chapter 16

Simon Saves the Day

■ ▬ ▬ ▬ ▬ ▬ ▬ ▬ ▬ ▬ ▬ ■

In the toy business, if you need three colors, they're always red, yellow, and blue. It's somewhere in the toy design Bible to use primary colors. If you need a fourth color, it's always green. Somehow purple and orange never get chosen for the fourth color. You gotta feel sorry for purple and orange, and never more so than when we developed the Simon game that debuted in 1978.

While I'm fascinated with mechanical objects and love to build them, I'm not skilled at electronic design. How does a GPS know where you are on the planet? How does a radio frequency tag know you went through a tollgate? How does an MRI see inside your body? All of these inventions are miracles. I love to discover how they function, but I don't know how to create them. My partner Howard Morrison, however, was a talented inventor who loved to play with electronic designs.

Howard was in the right place at the right time in the middle of the 1970s, when electronic games grew from a niche product into a mainstay of the toy industry. The idea for Simon, Howard's greatest invention, was generated in 1976 when he and fellow inventor Ralph Baer wandered into a trade show for arcade video games at the Conrad Hilton Hotel in Chicago.

Howard and Ralph came upon an arcade game called Touch Me, made by Atari, a game that had flopped when introduced to the public a couple of years earlier. Touch Me was an electronic memory game that generated a sequence of flashing lights and sounds to create a pattern that the player would follow by pushing the corresponding buttons on the panel. They were intrigued with the game but saw that it was badly designed. All the buttons were black and the sounds the toy emitted were harshly unpleasant. Despite the game's failure, Howard and Ralph saw something in the "flop." Howard realized that Touch Me was a fabulous concept with poor execution.

"The thing that frustrated me about that arcade game," explained Morrison, "was that it was in an environment that had so much other commotion going on around it, and this made an incredibly big strain on your memory.... And when I realized that, I thought to myself, *You know what? This has got to be done in the home.... It's got to be something that can challenge and challenge and challenge without all this distraction.* And that's when I came up with the idea," according to *Inside Marvin Glass's Toy Vault!*

After the arcade trade show, Howard Morrison came into my office and said, "Grab a pencil." On my desk sat my coffee cup, a glass of water, and a small plate. He instructed, "Do as I do and follow me." He tapped my coffee cup with his pencil; it made a little *ping* sound. He prompted me to do the same with my pencil and of course I got the same *ping*. Howard then struck the coffee cup, followed by my glass of water, so I heard a *ping* and then a *pang* sound. I followed with *ping* and *pang*. He again started from the beginning but added the small plate. Now we had *ping, pang,* and *dong*. I followed again. "Last one," he added, and went back to the coffee cup again for number four, so now we had *ping, pang, dong,* and *ping*. I said, "Let's do it."

Howard explained that Texas Instruments had developed a computer chip that combined all the elements of computing onto one small, inexpensive piece of silicon. He wanted to use the computer chip to electronically create the same results that he was demonstrating with his pencil. The computer chip would illuminate one of the four colored lights and simultaneously generate a musical tone. The player would then follow the pattern of blinking lights and sounds generated by the game. Howard said that Ralph could engineer the cutting-edge computer technology needed to make it work.

Ralph Baer was the chief engineer of Sanders Associates Inc. in Nashua, New Hampshire. Sanders was a military electronics research company specializing in tactical surveillance equipment. At Sanders in 1966, Ralph figured how to control a blip on a cathode ray tube, or, in other words, a television tube. Over the next six years, Baer worked on developing the first video game system. When he succeeded in 1972, Sanders had no interest in the video game business and licensed the technology to Magnavox.

Magnavox produced the Odyssey video game system, then licensed the technology to the founder of Atari, Nolan Bushnell, who developed the arcade game Pong in 1972. Pong, a two-dimensional table tennis game, made both a fortune and history. So much so that president George W. Bush presented Ralph Baer with the National Medal of Technology Award in 2006 for his pioneering creation, development, and commercialization of interactive video games. Ralph was a computer genius and a wonderful, kind man.

Howard Morrison explained how he built the prototype for his idea, which he called Feedback at the time. "When I did Simon," he recalled in *Inside Marvin Glass's Toy Vault!*, " I made a little square box, just a square box, with four square colored buttons and I called it Feedback. The buttons were red, yellow, blue, and green." Howard went on to describe how a little incandescent light bulb and a contact switch were positioned under each of the four colored buttons. The square box included an audio speaker and a cord that connected to an Apple computer. The square box prototype was simple, but the computer program that ran the Apple computer was not. Howard and Ralph developed the computer program along with a young software engineer, Lenny Cope.

Each of the four colored buttons was assigned a musical note: blue was E, yellow was C-sharp, red was A, and green was also an E, but an octave lower than the blue button. The tones of Simon were designed always to be harmonic. Ralph consulted with musicians and learned that a bugle produces only four notes, so the musical tones were based on a pleasing bugle call. Crucially, Simon always sounded great, regardless of what order the tones were played.

The player's goal was to follow and repeat the sequence of lights and sounds by pushing the corresponding buttons in the correct order. Howard designed the game so that if you correctly repeated six moves in a row, the pace of the game increased, creating more fun and tension. When you screwed up and pressed the wrong button, you got a loud razz sound, adding laughs to your loss. If you completed the entire sequence of thirty-two moves, you received a loud chorus of praise and a six-signal salute. Your brain received a shot of dopamine as a reward for your Simon victory. Howard explained, "I got the idea of having something that would always want to do you one better." Howard designed five variations of the game, so players could play the game alone or with partners.

We had to improve upon the square black box that housed the game, and our talented artistic designer, Doug Montague, dreamed up the futuristic spaceship design with the sleek black casing. The whole office played Feedback for weeks and weeks, perfecting all the little nuances of our fun and funny game before we were happy with the prototype (which was later sold as Simon). We arranged to present the game to Mel Taft, the vice president of research and development for Milton Bradley.

I'm not a baseball player, but growing up on the North Side of Chicago, I'm a Cubs fan. When you watch a baseball player swing the bat and make *that* connection, the batter knows in an instant when he's hit a homer. When we placed Feedback on the table in our conference room, we knew it was a home run before Mel even turned on the switch. We knew he would buy it the first time he touched the buttons and heard the sounds. Mel remembered, "When they showed it to me, I loved it! But you have to be so careful when Marvin or his people would demonstrate something to you, they'd be all enthusiastic and everything, and enthusiasm breeds enthusiasm," he explained in *Inside Marvin Glass's Toy Vault!* Mel bought it anyway.

Milton Bradley started production of Simon in March 1978 at their plant in Springfield, Massachusetts. Fortunately, the marketing team at Milton Bradley had changed the game's name from Feedback to Simon, a reference to the game Simon Says. It went on sale in April and immediately started disappearing off the shelves. Simon broke all the rules, because it was a relatively expensive game, selling between twenty and forty dollars, which was a lot of money then. It was also selling well without any nationally televised commercials. Milton Bradley's vice president explained, "By the end of April, we were starting to sense that this was a unique situation," reported the *Chicago Tribune* in 1978.

Just a few months earlier, on November 18, 1977, Steven Spielberg had released *Close Encounters of the Third Kind.* Spielberg's movie was a blockbuster. In it, a circular alien spaceship communicates with people by playing a sequence of musical notes and flashing lights. The similarities between *Close Encounters* and Simon were coincidental, but they helped buyers recognize the toy when it hit the shelves. Spielberg later claimed that we stole the idea for Simon from his movie, but Howard had filed for his patent on September 19, 1977. Ralph Baer and Howard Morrison shared the credit on the patent.

Milton Bradley threw a fabulous celebrity-filled party at Studio 54 in New York City to celebrate Simon's success on May 15, 1978. Studio 54 was a sensational, world-famous nightclub that opened in 1977 when disco music was the rage. Customers waited in line for hours to get into the club at 254 W. 54th Street. The Simon celebration was the only time I partied at Studio 54. It was a great bash and Milton-Bradley paid for all the MGA partners to stay at the Waldorf Astoria Hotel. The celebrities included dancer Mikhail Baryshnikov, Broadway and movie star Carol Channing, and singer Stephanie Mills. Along with others, they all participated in Milton Bradley's "Simon Celebrity Challenge."

The 1978 television commercial was a classic. Four young adults surround the Simon game as it sits on a table and a party rocks in the background. The actor Vincent Price speaks in a jaunty voice over the sounds of beeps and party noise. Price chants in his deep voice, "Simon sets the pace, you follow right along. Light the lights that Simon lights or he'll tell you that you're wrong. Simon's a computer, Simon has a brain. You either do what Simon says or else go down the drain. Simon is a master. He tells you what to do. But you can master Simon if you follow every clue. And if you think that Simon is fun at a party, wait until you play it alone!"

Simon was a blockbuster for Milton Bradley and MGA. The game was on the cover of *Newsweek* on December 11, 1978, for their story "Turned-On Toys." By the end of 1982, Simon had sold ten million units in the first four years and earned $9 million for MGA. Simon was a bases-loaded, bottom-of-the-ninth, seventh-game-World-Series-winning, grand-slam home run.

One of the unexpected benefits of Simon was its impact on education and medical therapy. Teachers wrote and told us how helpful it was to students, particularly those with eye problems, who watched the lights flash and listened to the tones. Nursing homes wrote in and described how Simon stimulated older people's memories and what a boon it was in memory therapy. Many years later, Howard himself used Simon to help recover his memory after a bad motorcycle accident left him with amnesia. We were delighted to learn our toy had a positive impact on the teaching and medical fields.

Simon was the most iconic of all the toys and games created by Marvin Glass & Associates, and variations of Simon have continued to be introduced since it debuted in 1978. Milton Bradley introduced Super Simon and Pocket Simon in 1980. Hasbro bought out Milton Bradley in 1984, and they unveiled Simon Trickster in 2005, Simon Swipe in 2014, Simon Air in 2016 and Simon Optix in 2017. Just as Marvin had done in the 1950s with his toy dogs and in the 1960s with his plastic robots, manufacturers kept the ball rolling. When they saw a good thing, they stuck with it. In 2006, *Smithsonian* magazine wrote that Simon "ushered in the era of electronic games."

Simon's smash success brought new energy and enthusiasm to MGA after the terrible ordeal of the shootings. We would never forget our pain and losses from that awful day, but Simon's amazing success reminded us that we were a dynamic company in a fabulous industry. Simon was the game that made the cover of *Newsweek*. Simon was the game that got me into Studio 54 in New York City without waiting in line. We were back.

The annual New York Toy Fair is where the rubber meets the road in the U.S. toy industry. It's here where fortunes are made and dreams are crushed. Hundreds of thousands of toys are on display for retailers in the glass-walled Javits Convention Center on Manhattan's West Side. If the major retailers buy a toy from the manufacturers, it will go into production and be sold to the public. If a toy fails to sell here, every cent invested in the product is lost. Our financial fate was tied directly to the toy manufacturers. When they made money, so did we. When they didn't, we didn't.

Most of the partners and I attended the New York Toy Fair every February. All of our customers displayed their new toys and games here. Some years we brought a designer or model maker with us to New York as a reward for their outstanding work. The partners always had a hard time deciding who should be selected, because everyone at MGA wanted to come to the toy fair. It was hard not to have fun in New York, but I usually left these fairs feeling conflicted—both exhilarated and a bit depressed. Only a handful of toys presented at the fair succeeded, and I wondered how some of them could be ours. When I returned to Chicago after attending a toy fair, I would often stop work on some of our projects because they were too similar to designs I had seen on display.

As our business expanded, we sold more products around the world, and I traveled to more international toy fairs. Occasionally, I visited toy shows in Hong Kong and Tokyo, and often traveled to London and Paris, but I *never* missed Nuremberg.

The Germans are fanatics about toys, games, models, and puzzles. The Spielwarenmesse in Nuremberg is the largest and most fabulous toy fair in the world. Held annually since 1949, their fair is open only to the trade. About eighty thousand people attend the six-day event, where exhibitors from scores of countries display about one million products. The huge exhibition hall contains multiple buildings, some of which are devoted to only one type of product. One building displays nothing but miniature model trains—incredible.

The German jigsaw puzzle business dwarfs the output of U.S. manufacturers. Ravensburger, the powerhouse of the German puzzle business, makes a product that is hard to believe until you see it—the world's largest jigsaw puzzle. It contains an unbelievable 33,600 pieces and when finished measures 19 feet long by 5 feet wide. The puzzle arrives in ten separate bags, each containing one section. You can assemble each section and then combine them to complete the puzzle, or, if you want a real challenge, you can mix up all ten bags before you begin. Some people actually do mix all 33,600 pieces together before they start working on this eccentric, time-consuming, exceptionally complex challenge.

One of my favorite things about visiting international toy fairs was meeting interesting people. The other toymakers and I bonded over our common desire to make great products for children. Toys and games transcend language and culture. What entertains and amuses children is universal. Children's play patterns are similar everywhere—even other mammals share them. Watch any dog or cat playing with a ball or empty box. It's instinctive.

I traveled extensively and established many friendships in the toy business. We all made toys designed to entertain and educate children, and every adult could relate to that. When I flew, I always made sure the person sitting next to me told me about their work first, because once we started discussing toys, we wouldn't stop until the end of the flight. Everyone had stories about their favorite toy, their favorite Christmas present, the games they would play for hours as a kid. I loved the toy business and enjoyed its universal appeal when I navigated the globe.

The most important and remarkable trip I ever took, however, was to the Soviet Union in 1981. And it had nothing to do with the toy business.

Chapter 17

The Soviet Union and the KGB

etween June 5 and June 10, 1967, Israel defeated Egypt, Jordan, and Syria in what became known as the Six-Day War. It was a brilliant and unlikely military success for many reasons, not the least of which was that Israel's enemies had much larger armies and used Soviet weaponry. Immediately, life in the USSR became more difficult for Jews than it had been before the war. Jews were routinely subjected to extreme harassment and intimidation.

Thousands of Jews applied for exit visas to leave the Soviet Union. Most of them wanted to immigrate to Israel or the United States. The government refused most of the exit visas and many applicants were fired from their jobs. These Jews, known as Refuseniks, gave up everything to leave. Refuseniks were often forced to live in poverty and move into communal apartments with strangers, sometimes sharing one bathroom and kitchen. Refuseniks had no legal rights and became "nonpersons" in the deadening vernacular of the Soviet Union. The Cold War was in full swing and the plight of the Soviet Jews became a well-known international story.

In 1978, Chicago Action for Soviet Jewry (CASJ) was formed in Highland Park, IL under the charismatic leadership of Pam Cohen and Marilyn Tallman. Their primary goal was to exert political pressure to help the Refuseniks leave the Soviet Union. Cohen and Tallman organized massive letter-writing campaigns and arranged for Jewish "tourists" to visit Refuseniks in the USSR. These "tourists" brought cameras, film, medicines, and clothing to help the Refuseniks survive by providing them with goods they could sell on the black market.

Marlene and I joined CASJ in the late '70s, along with two other couples who lived in Highland Park, Jackie and Harvey Barnett, and Susan and Gary Gurvey. All of us were dear friends who had attended the University of Illinois together in the early '60s—we also shared Russian ancestry. After watching the harsh situation unfold in the USSR for several years, the six of us grew angry and decided to take direct and personal action. We would travel together to the Soviet Union and visit Refuseniks as "tourists" in 1981.

Working with Chicago Action for Soviet Jewry, we studied together for three months in a clandestine process. The CASJ assigned twenty families to each couple. The Refuseniks lived in Leningrad, Moscow, and Kiev. We were told we would visit six or seven families in each city. During those three months we amassed medicine, clothing, and electronic goods to give them to help them survive while they waited for permission to emigrate. Some Jewish families waited many years to leave the Soviet Union. Some never were allowed to leave.

We were instructed that we would all travel together from city to city and stay in the same hotel. During the day, each couple would travel separately to visit our assigned families. At night we would come together to eat dinner. We were told to memorize the family names and addresses. I wrote down three lists in tiny lettering, one for each city, of the names, addresses, and "gifts" for each family. I laminated each list and hid them inside fake business cards, which I could then peel open when we arrived in Moscow, Leningrad, or Kiev.

It was risky for American citizens to travel to the USSR and visit "nonpersons" at the height of the Cold War. Our three months of preparation and study were stressful, but my dear friend Harvey Barnett had already been on a trip to the USSR to provide aid to the Refuseniks. He told us it was one of the most incredible experiences of his life, and I believed him—that's why Marlene and I were going. Harvey gave us strength to carry on with our plan.

When I told my father what we were planning, he thought I was crazy. He reminded me that I had sons who were twelve, nine, and four. I reminded him that his father, Jacob, had left Kiev alone when he was only seventeen to come to America to make a new life. It was in America that Jacob met Minnie and raised a family. At that, my dad smiled and wished me good luck and safe travels. Marlene told her mother only that we were taking a trip to Europe. Marlene didn't want her mother to know the truth because she didn't want her to worry about us on our adventure.

We packed extra-large suitcases when we prepared to fly to the Soviet Union. We crammed each one full of dozens of items to give away, and I could barely lift them when we were done packing. I also purchased a new Sony Betamax video camera that weighed close to ten pounds. It had a fraction of the resolution of today's electronics, but it worked. I planned to carry the Betamax in my shoulder bag, but I would only use it if a Refusenik was comfortable with being interviewed.

Everyone was nervous and concerned when we landed at the Moscow airport. We weren't carrying anything illegal, but we were bringing in four huge suitcases filled with extra clothing, medicine, and electronic goods—supposedly what two adults would want while traveling for ten days in the USSR. No one would be fooled if customs decided to inspect our bags, so we were relieved when we all passed through unchecked. Because of our extra-large suitcases, each couple had to take their own taxi to our hotel.

The drive from the airport was bleak and depressing. Heavy rain fell. Mile after mile of run-down apartment buildings lined the road. The old buildings looked like they were about to collapse. As I looked out the window and realized there had been no new building construction in years, I was shocked.

The taxi's windshield wipers were flipping back and forth like crazy, trying to keep up with the downpour. All of a sudden, one wiper flew right off the windshield. Our driver instantly stopped the car, jumped out into the downpour, and went in search of his missing wiper. He was smiling when he got back into the car, drenched but holding the wiper blade. He explained that it was impossible to buy spare parts for cars, and even if you could, it took forever. Welcome to Moscow, circa 1981.

We had no scheduled appointments when we set out to visit our assigned families. We just showed up on their doorstep and knocked. None of the families knew when we would show up; they just knew that someday we would. They had all been in contact with Pam Cohen and Marilyn Tallman from Chicago Action for Soviet Jewry, who arranged everything. We brought them goods, but we also brought them information and hope that the outside world was aware of their plight and they were not forgotten. The political pressure of CASJ also made them safer—the Soviet government couldn't simply make them disappear without our finding out about it. Our arrival was a cause for immediate celebration among the Refuseniks. We were welcomed like long-lost family, with smiles and hugs, wine, vodka, and cheese. We also had plenty to talk about! And thankfully, everyone spoke English.

All of the Refuseniks we met were professionals—engineers, doctors, accountants, and teachers—but they were no longer allowed to work or travel. They described the hardships they had endured after they applied to emigrate. The Refuseniks were prepared to suffer while they waited for permission to leave the country. Everyone talked about their dreams of living in freedom in the United States or Israel.

In turn, we shared stories about how our parents or grandparents got to the United States. Three of my grandparents came from Russia, and my father's mother, Minnie, came from Belarus. Sitting in these cramped apartments, I realized that if my grandparents hadn't left Russia, I could be one of these people confined to an apartment, waiting and hoping for freedom.

We provided each family with clothes, electronics, and medicines. Like everything else, Pam and Marilyn in Highland Park knew which medicines each family needed. And when we returned, we brought back additional information to Pam and Marilyn about the needs of new Refuseniks. All of the goods we gave them could be sold on the black market to get money to buy food. One simple 35 mm camera with film could bring in enough money to feed a family of four for a year. When we parted, we cried and spoke of our hopes of someday seeing each other again in the United States or Israel.

I did meet a few Jews in the Soviet Union who were not Refuseniks, but they were always afraid of the KGB and of losing what they had. Once people crossed the line and applied for permission to leave, their lives were awful, but they were no longer terrified.

We used the Moscow subway system to get around. It was impressive—the deepest subway in the world at 243 feet underground. You just kept going down escalator after escalator. One day on the subway, a KGB agent followed Marlene and me. It was easy to identify us as Americans. Speaking English and wearing Western clothes, we stood out like two beacons in the night. The KGB man, dressed in a trench coat, thin black tie, and black hat, was right out of central casting. His attire was like a costume. He kept staring at us, wanting us to know we were being followed.

His blatant attempt to intimidate us annoyed me, and we decided to shake him off. We got off at the next stop, crossed the platform to the other side, and got on the next train going back the way we came. He did the same thing. I told Marlene to stand next to the exit but not to leave the train. We waited until the rest of the passengers got off and let the new group get on. Then, as soon as everyone boarded, we quickly got off the train right before the doors closed. The station was nearly empty, and when we looked down the platform, we didn't see the KGB man. We won this round of cat and mouse in Moscow.

After meeting with our Moscow families, we flew to Leningrad first class on Aeroflot, the Soviet state airline. There were no jetways, so we walked on the tarmac to a stairway that led up to the plane, a twin-engine turbo-prop that looked like an old beat-up DC-3. I guessed it was Soviet-made, but it looked like a Douglas aircraft from the late 1930s.

It was a strange flight. When they called for first-class passengers, we moved ahead but discovered there were no seat assignments. First class meant only that you boarded the plane first and had your choice of open seats. The plane was one big cabin and all the seats were the same. We learned that first class was for Westerners. After we boarded, the Soviet citizens were allowed to board until the plane filled up. Passengers who couldn't get a seat returned to the terminal and waited for the next flight. We thought it was bizarre to treat your own people as second-class citizens.

When Marlene and I traveled to help Refuseniks in 1981, the city of St. Petersburg was called Leningrad. It had originally been called St. Petersburg after tsar Peter the Great, who founded the city in 1703 on the shores of the Baltic Sea, directly across from Finland. The city, renamed Petrograd in 1914, was the capital of Russia for more than 200 years, until the capital was transferred to Moscow in 1918, a year after the Russian Revolution. In January 1924, the city's name was changed to Leningrad in honor of Soviet leader Vladimir Lenin, who had died earlier that month. In 1991, after the collapse of the Soviet Union, the name of the city was changed back to St. Petersburg. It's a Westernized city because of its proximity to Europe and boasts spectacular cultural treasures such as the Hermitage Museum and the Summer Palace. Sightseeing, however, was not on our agenda. We saw none of it.

The Gonsky family lived in Leningrad. After applying to emigrate, they were forced to move into a shared apartment and live with two other families. They were the only family we visited who had young children, two daughters about eight and six. The four of them lived in one room that was about ten feet square. The two girls slept on a single mattress on the floor and the parents in a single bed. All of their clothes and posses-sions were in boxes. They had a few pots and cooking utensils, and when it was their turn, they took their food to the kitchen to prepare it. They ate in their room. They had no refrigerator and had to shop daily.

I asked the father, Yuri Gonsky, if he could afford a better apartment. He said yes but the government wouldn't give him permission to move. He was virtually a prisoner in his own country because he was a Jew who wanted to emigrate. I gave Yuri a simple 35 mm camera and some film. He thanked me profusely and told me he would sell it the next day on the black market. When it was time for us to leave, we parted with hugs and tears. Yuri and his family were eventually released and made it to Israel.

Another Refusenik we called on was Arkady Verlinski. He had written a history of the Jewish cemetery in Leningrad and wanted to get it to a friend of his who was now in Israel. The only way I could smuggle out the document was by photographing it with my 35 mm camera. I shot eight rolls of film. Months later, I managed to get a copy of Verlinski's historical document to his friend in Tel Aviv.

The final city on our agenda was Kiev, in the far west of the USSR. Kiev is now the capital of Ukraine. My grandfather Jacob came from this ancient city that sits on the banks of the Dnieper River. Unfortunately, Jacob died when I was twenty-one and I had never thought to ask about his Russian childhood or how he managed to escape as a young man.

Kiev is the most naturally beautiful of the three cities and sports lovely grounds and parks. We stayed at the Dnieper Hotel on the river. We were warned during training to be extra careful while in Kiev, because some people who had traveled there in the past thought they had been followed, although nothing had happened to anyone. Initially, we didn't have much reason for concern.

Our last visit was with Lev Dudkin and his family. The Dudkins were outspoken and cavalier when they became Refuseniks, which concerned me, but I loved his family immediately. When I showed him my Betamax video camera, popped out the cassette, and explained that you could watch the tape immediately on your television, Lev said it sounded like a miracle. I agreed. He assured me it had to be the first video camera in Kiev and possibly all of the Soviet Union. He might have been right.

Lev was my best interview of the trip. He loved to talk and was over-joyed when I told him we represented Chicago Action for Soviet Jewry. He had heard of Pam Cohen and Marilyn Tallman in Highland Park and the fabulous work they were doing on behalf of the Refuseniks.

On our last night, the six of us from CASJ ate dinner in Kiev and shared stories about our incredible experiences. It was an amazing but exhausting trip, and we were all ready to get home and see our families. We remembered we were in Kiev, however, and kept our voices low and never mentioned names. It was easy to become paranoid after eight days in the communist Soviet Union.

The next morning, we prepared to fly from Kiev to Moscow, where we would connect with a flight back home. Marlene and I only had one suitcase left. We had given the other three away along with all of our goods. Marlene had also given away her winter fur coat.

As we were getting ready to leave the hotel, the phone rang. I an-swered. It was the manager, who spoke good English, and she asked, "Could you please come to my office?" When I asked her if there was a problem with the bill, she replied curtly that she just needed to talk with me. I told Marlene I needed to see the manager and reassured her that it must be about the bill.

I found the manager's office and saw a heavyset woman sitting at a desk. To her right was a couch with two KGB men sitting on it. Just like the guys in Moscow, they were dressed right out of central casting, with the same black thin ties and somber expressions. The manager motioned for me to sit on another couch to her left facing them. She didn't intro-duce us and told me these men needed to talk with me.

My heart jumped into high gear and I instantly broke into a sweat as I sat down. I thought, *Oh shit. I'm fucked.* Fortunately, we had received some training before we left Highland Park on how to behave if we were brought in for interrogation.

One of the guys started talking to the manager in Russian, who translated, "We understand you have been visiting nonpersons. Who told you to see these people?"

As instructed, I replied, "I'm a tourist in your beautiful city; I have no idea what you are talking about." She continued, "We understand you have been visiting people in their homes." I responded, "I have no idea what you are talking about. We have enjoyed being in Kiev." As the manager translated, I was sure that these two goons understood every word I said.

The second guy jumped in with a raised voice and glared at me. The manager angrily translated, "Not only have you been visiting these nonpersons but you have been interviewing them and taking movies of them in their apartments!" I was fucked. I realized the KGB had bugged Lev Dudkin's apartment and listened to our entire conversation. They knew about the Betamax. "We are going up to your room right now to see your camera."

With that, the two KGB men got up and headed for the elevator. The manager and I trailed behind. The elevator was painfully tight for the four of us, and when the door opened, I was the first one out. I told the manager my wife was undressed and they would have to wait a minute before entering the room. Marlene already had her clothes on when I'd left the room, but I needed a moment to talk to her. I opened the door slightly and quickly closed it behind me. "They're here outside the door," I whispered. "KGB. Please don't say a word and let me handle this." Marlene was visibly shocked and frightened.

I heard pounding on the door and grabbed my shoulder bag containing the Betamax camera with the videotape, the 35 mm camera, and all my canisters of Kodak exposed film. When I opened the door, the manager looked at my bag and said the four of us would have to return to her office. I was starting to get angry at being accused of being a villain and a "spy."

The second KGB guy asked me to remove the film from the video camera. I pushed the button and the motor inside opened and popped out the video cassette. I put it on the manager's desk. I knew none of them had ever seen anything like this. The questioning resumed.

"Who told you to visit these nonpersons?" He again used this horrible description of our new friends and I knew I could no longer deny our visits. "The people we visited were *persons*," I said to the manager. "Tell him we were visiting people."

"Who told you to visit them?"

"Our rabbi." It was the answer we were trained to respond if we were ever in this situation.

"What's your rabbi's name?"

We had been taught to "make up any name you can."

I said, "Sam Goldstein." It sounded like a good name for a rabbi.

"Who were you visiting?" came next. I made up a Russian-sounding name.

He knew that I was lying. Their next move shocked me. The KGB men cleared off the top of the manager's desk. Then they opened my shoulder bag and methodically removed all my gear and put it on the desk. They lined up my Betamax camera, 35 mm camera, and all of the exposed film canisters. Then they ordered me to sit in the manager's chair behind the desk. At this point I was angry and scared. I thought about my sons and Siberia and wondered if I was going to get out of Kiev and the USSR.

I dumbly took my seat, and when I looked up, saw that a third KGB man had entered the room. He had placed a camera on a tripod. As I sat at the desk behind my "spy" paraphernalia, all I could think was, *I'm really fucked now.* In English, the photographer said, "Look at the camera," and started snapping away. I couldn't imagine what would happen next.

The second KGB man placed a piece of blank paper and a pen in front of me. In English, he said, "Write that you apologize to the Soviet Union for visiting these nonpersons."

I wrote and left out the "non."

"Write down the name of your rabbi."

I wrote down "Sam Goldstein."

"Who did you visit?"

I made up a name but he knew I was lying.

"Do you have any more film for this movie camera upstairs in your room?"

I told him, "No, it's my only film."

"If you have any more film you are trying to take out of this country, we will find it when you are at the airport in Moscow, and they will bring you back to Kiev."

I was surprised when he said, "You can go now." He confiscated only the Betamax cassette tape and told me to take everything else. I wasn't too concerned about the video because I doubted anyone in the country had a Betamax player.

I left the office with my bag full of gear and ran into Gary Gurvey and Harvey Barnett in the lobby. Gary had also just been interviewed, but they hadn't questioned Harvey, which actually upset him. Harvey was a trial lawyer back in Chicago and wanted to be interrogated by the KGB. The three of us walked across to the park so we could talk freely. We tried to guess what was next and decided to leave immediately for the airport. We told the desk that we needed three taxis to take us to the airport. It was only a few minutes before three black cars drove up. But they weren't taxis. The KGB goons drove us to the airport in a ride that I thought might never end.

We flew out of Kiev without incident and arrived at the Moscow airport. When we got to security and the agent saw the name "Breslow" on our passports, he called a supervisor. They took us aside and searched every inch of our luggage for another "movie film." When they didn't find one, Marlene and I were allowed to leave with the rest of my gear and film. In the end, they only confiscated the videotape in Kiev.

Our trip to the USSR had been stressful and scary, but it was also a joyous celebration for all of us. Everyone we visited was finally released. It took five or six years for some families to emigrate to Israel or the United States. I managed to keep in touch with Lev Dudkin, from our last meeting in Kiev, and I flew out to see him when he arrived in Boston. He told me that the day after we departed Kiev, a photo of me with my camera gear was on the front page of the newspaper. The paper reported that an American spy, Jeffrey Breslow, was visiting nonpersons in Kiev. I was happy and relieved when he told me his family hadn't suffered any repercussions from our visit.

My father was proud of me when I told him about our Soviet adventure. He thought it was courageous for us to help fellow Jews who were being persecuted for wanting to leave the USSR to start a new life. My dad told me my Grandpa Jacob would have been proud of me as well.

Chapter 18

Electronic Toys Explode and
Teenage Mutant Ninja Turtles (Not)

I faced a busy studio when I returned to work after my risky sojourn to the USSR in 1981. MGA was thriving, but we were facing a massive transformation in the toy industry—the sweeping tide of electronics and computers into toys and games. The electronic Simon game had bailed out MGA and brought us back to life just a few years before, so we were enthusiastic believers in the unlimited possibilities of electronic toys—no one more so than partner Howard Morrison.

In 1980, a Japanese company named Namco developed the precursor to one of the highest-grossing games in history, Pac-Man. Namco's video arcade game was called Puck Man. It was a mediocre coin-operated game with simple graphics that showed up on the screen as a hockey puck with a triangular piece missing, eating away in a maze. The hot games in Japan then were Space Invaders and other shooting contests. Puck Man wasn't a hit there, but it appealed to girls in a way that none of the shooting games did.

A Chicago company saw the potential in the game and acquired the rights to Puck Man from Namco. Midway, a division of Bally Manufacturing, licensed the game from Namco. Midway dramatically improved the graphics and changed its name from Puck Man to Pac-Man. They were afraid that kids would change the *P* in Puck to an *F* by scratching away some paint.

Pac-Man is still regarded by toy designers as the most influential game of all time. Midway/Bally had found their Simon. When the game was released, their numbers were astronomical—Pac-Man brought in ten *billion* quarters. They sold more than 350,000 arcade cabinets at $2,400 each in the first eighteen months of release, earning almost a billion dollars. Never before or since has the coin-op business seen anything like it. Pac-Man proved the value of video games and opened up that world to girls and women.

We noticed that *Pac-Man* was developed by a Chicago company and, of course, decided that we would start designing our own coin-op video games, even though they were expensive and time-consuming to develop. The development time in the coin-op arcade design business was four to six months and very costly. We could put a plastic mock-up of a toy or game on the conference room table in a day and show the concept, but that wasn't possible in the video game business. We also learned to *never underestimate* what a kid can do in a video arcade.

We hired a software developer and installed computers, and Howard and the software designer set to work. Their first effort, called Domino Man, flopped in 1982. So did their second, Tapper, in 1983. We felt sure that their third invention, Clone, was going to be our Pac-Man.

All video arcade games at that time allowed you to enter your three initials if you achieved a high score. Your high score got you on the screen and knocked out the "low man on the totem pole," so to speak. It was the player's reward for pumping hundreds of quarters into that particular box.

Clone had a small inexpensive black-and-white camera on top of the case. When you popped in your quarter, you were prompted to look up at the camera and take a picture of your face. Your face now appeared on the screen, inside one of the organic-looking pods that you could control while moving it around. Floating around on the screen were other pods that were shooting at you. The faces in these other pods were digital photographs of the high-scoring players who had played the game before you. When you shot another pod in the correct place, your face replaced the previous player's face. You tried to clone yourself as many times as you could. If you got a high score, your face would stay in the machine until another player replaced your face with theirs. For the early '80s, this was advanced and very cool technology.

Essentially, the Clone game took a selfie of the player, long before cell phones were taking high-quality photographs. The Clone camera took black-and-white photos of decent quality. We anticipated that young teenage boys might try to get another image on the Clone pod instead of their face—for instance, a middle finger. We even thought a boy might bring in a photo from *Playboy* or some other magazine, so we put a button on the back of the game box that allowed the proprietor to erase any obscene images. We thought our potential problem was solved.

In the coin-op arcade business, you first build one machine and install it in one location. If it brings in the quarters, you have a hit, and if not, it means you blew six months of development and lots of money. We excitedly installed Clone in one of Chicago's western suburbs. It operated in place for one week before something happened that we'd *never, ever* considered. Two teenage boys went into the arcade and put a quarter into the Clone game. When the game prompted the player to take a face photo, one of the boys took off his pants and underwear and somehow kneeled on his friend's shoulders so the machine took a black-and-white picture of his penis. That was his photo for the Clone pod.

The proprietor unplugged the machine and called us to remove it from the arcade. If our Clone game was somehow encouraging kids to get naked to take obscene photos in his arcade, he wanted nothing to do with it. Our Clone experiment was over.

We decided to try to salvage Clone by removing the camera and reinventing it as the Journey game, based on the band. The object of the Journey game was to reunite the members of the band with their instruments and lead singer Steve Perry with his microphone. The game had the faces of each band member placed on a cartoon body. If this sounds horrible, it was. In 2007, *Game Informer* magazine named the Journey game number 9 on its "Top 10 Worst Game Ideas" (ever). The best part of the game is that we had Journey's music on a cassette player in the cabinet playing their music.

MGA and Midway, who were partners on the game, needed the final approval of the Journey band members before proceeding. Journey was playing for a few nights in 1982 at the Salt Palace in Salt Lake City, so Midway flew the arcade game out there and it was set up backstage. Marlene, Marc, Michael, Joey (who was just five), and I flew out to Salt Lake City too, and before the concert we went backstage and played the game with all the members of the band. Meeting Steve Perry and getting autographs was a big thrill for Marc, who was twelve years old. The concert was great and the band liked the game, but all in all, it was a sad attempt at trying to save the Clone game.

When the Journey game struck out, we decided the coin-op game business was not for Marvin Glass & Associates. In 1985, two of our employees, Rich and Elaine Ditton, left MGA to start Incredible Technologies in the basement of their home. Today, they have a string of hit arcade games and 130 employees, and they've been incredibly successful. When we were closing down our video game business, I kept thinking of Kenny Rogers singing his song "The Gambler." We knew when to walk away, and we knew when to run—and we did.

We made the right choice when we walked away from Clone and electronic games, but I was about to make the worst decision of my career. And I mean *colossally* bad. In 1985, when I was forty-two and had been running MGA for nine years, one of our young designers was into comic books in a big way. I don't remember his name—I think it's too painful to remember. Let's call him Tim.

I didn't enjoy comic books and hadn't read one since I was ten. But one day, Tim came into my office to tell me about an underground comic book he was reading and collecting. He explained that it was a little bizarre but that he thought it might work in the toy industry. He didn't bring a copy with him but said he'd bring one in the next day. I asked him to go ahead and tell me about it as long as he was sitting there. He mentioned again that it was "weird," and I replied, "I can listen to weird." Slowly, so that I would catch each word, Tim enunciated, "It's called *Teenage...Mutant...Ninja...Turtles.*" I said, "You're kidding." I might even have said, "You're fucking kidding."

Tim continued, "The four main characters are turtles named after four Italian Renaissance artists. The first is Donatello; the next is Leonardo, as in da Vinci; the third is Michelangelo; and the last is Raphael." He started to explain who they were until I cut him off: "I know who they are." Tim said their names were shortened to Donnie, Leo, Mickey, and Ralph. Now I definitely said, "You're fucking kidding me."

I thought Tim should get back to work, but he wanted to continue, so I let him. He told me the turtles were trained in martial arts by a New York sewer rat sensei, and they battled criminals, mutated creatures, and alien invaders, all while trying to remain hidden from society. I was annoyed by then and told Tim, "We design toys for children—for Fisher-Price, Barbie, Hot Wheels, and *Sesame Street* characters. You're suggesting ninja turtles named after the most brilliant artists and sculptors the world has ever known, trained by a New York sewer rat. Why not toy mud-wrestling pigs called Mozart, Bach, and Beethoven? Tim, you don't have to bring in the comic book. I think it's time for you to get back to work." If only I could take back those words!

Teenage Mutant Ninja Turtles (TMNT) went on to generate not hundreds of millions but BILLIONS of dollars of revenue over the next thirty years. TMNT was created by Kevin Eastman and Peter Laird and first published by Mirage Studios in Dover, New Hampshire. Today, I can laugh at myself and admire Mark Friedman, the licensing agent who sought out Eastman and Laird and signed them up to create the world of TMNT. I tip my "shell" to these men's brilliance.

I also give credit to the brilliant designers at Playmates Toys, founded in Hong Kong in 1966. Their designers noticed what I missed, because I'd never taken the time to look for it—the "dark" humor in the masked and armed green turtles who walk on two legs, brandish swords and spears, and speak English.

In 1988, Playmate Toys introduced TMNT action figures, soon branching out to vehicles, playsets, and puzzles. There were TMNT feature movies, television shows, video games, clothes, costumes, breakfast cereal, and pudding. There were waffle makers, rugs, pillows, and lunch bags. They performed in theaters, including the "Coming Out of Their Shells" musical tour. Pizza Hut jumped on the TMNT bandwagon as a sponsor, and so then the Turtles started eating pizza. The Turtles even created a hit single called "Pizza Power." I remember slowly walking through the Playmates Toys showroom at the New York Toy Fair and feeling sick. I walked past the Turtles at the European toy shows and felt sick there too. They were everywhere.

Even Lego succumbed to the lure of licensing the Turtles, and when my grandsons were little boys, I played TMNT Legos with them. The little Lego Turtle characters were just over an inch high. I asked my grandsons, Oscar and Jax, which Turtle was which because I couldn't tell them apart. They were surprised and explained that Leonardo had one color mask and Donatello had a different color of shell top, like this should be obvious to any intelligent person on the planet. I only hope when my grandsons read this that they get a laugh at how their Poppy missed out on this really big toy. I hope Mark Friedman, Kevin Eastman, and Peter Laird are enjoying flying on their private jets to their island homes in Fiji or Bora Bora. Good for them.

Chapter 19

Launching a New Company and *Trump: The Game*

D espite my screw-up by passing on TMNT, in the 1980s I was blessed with a great career and a happy home life. Howard Morrison, Rouben Terzian, and I had made a great team since we all started working together as toy designers at MGA in 1967. The most important element in our working relationship was celebrating our talents. We recognized and played to our strengths and avoided our weaknesses.

Howard Morrison was a thoughtful, kind, and wonderful man whom everyone loved. He was also an incredibly prolific and talented inventor. Howard, however, was a terrible businessman. He freely admitted it. He was a lousy poker player and couldn't keep his truthful mouth shut. I once told him that you never have to lie to a client, but you also don't have to tell them everything. Sometimes, we would show a fresh toy design to a few customers who rejected it. Then, while we were presenting the same product to someone new, Howard would tell the prospective client how many previous customers had already rejected the design. Howard and I had a discussion about his sales techniques, after which he left the business part to me.

Rouben Terzian was a mechanical genius who loved to work on dolls. Rouben, however, struggled to get along with clients and sometimes didn't relate well to other employees. He was also a perfectionist who took forever to finish a design. But he always pushed me to be more aggressive with clients and was never satisfied with the deal. I was the one who had to ask the customer for more money, but Rouben's assertiveness always worked to our financial advantage.

I was a skillful game designer and an excellent businessman, leading MGA to many profitable years. But I didn't always connect as well as I wanted to with other employees. I cared about them and was friendly but also quiet. When people felt they needed help and advice, they inevitably turned to Howard.

In 1988, after twenty-one years working at MGA, things changed. Marvin Glass had drawn up a partnership agreement sixteen years earlier that forced us to shut down MGA that year. Back in 1972, when Anson Isaacson became MGA's last full partner, Marvin rewrote our partnership agreement for the last time. The agreement allowed retired partners, their widows, and their heirs to continue receiving royalty income in perpetuity. This was terrific for them but ultimately toxic for the continuation of the company. By 1988, more than 60 percent of the income from new products was going to retired and nonworking partners.

But Marvin had created the 1972 agreement with an end point in mind: at the time, there were ten active partners at MGA, but the agreement stipulated that when, eventually, only three of the ten original partners remained active in the company, MGA must be dissolved. I think Marvin designed it that way because he believed the company couldn't succeed without him.

By 1988, only four partners remained active. Then Harry Disko, who had kept MGA's "little black book" of job numbers for three decades, decided to retire. Soon there would be only three original partners left—Howard Morrison, Rouben Terzian, and me. Under the terms of the 1972 partnership agreement, Harry's retirement forced MGA to close.

The ten partners or their estates would continue to collect royalties on all the existing MGA licenses, but there would no new products—or new sources of income—generated. It was a traumatic time, and there was a lot of acrimony between the three of us who remained and the retired partners, but it was the end for Marvin Glass & Associates.

MGA's partnership agreement didn't contain a noncompete clause, so Howard, Rouben, and I started our own toy design company immediately. We had seen the writing on the wall when Harry told us he was retiring and had been planning our new business for months. We reached out to our clients and got their support. They agreed that as long as we continued designing great toys and games, they would continue buying them from us.

MGA employed about seventy people when we closed, which was a considerable overhead. The three of us wanted to operate as a smaller company, and we couldn't take everyone with us anyway. We asked only the twenty-five employees who fit best in our company to join our new venture. Understandably, the forty-five people we didn't take with us were upset and angry. It was a difficult situation, but we forged ahead.

In May 1988, we launched our new toy design studio, Breslow, Morrison, Terzian & Associates. I thought we sounded like a law firm, but Rouben insisted we use our last names for the company. I didn't agree and thought we should adopt a fun name, but I acquiesced because Rouben was adamant. Our names were listed alphabetically, so mine came first. Just like International Business Machines became known as IBM, from day one, our clients and employees called us BMT. The three of us were equal partners.

BMT leased a 12,000-square-foot space on the sixth and top floor of a loft building at 750 N. Orleans Street on the Near North Side. We were just three blocks west of our old MGA building. We wanted to be on one floor because we felt that the two-story design at MGA had been inefficient. We also eliminated individual offices and opted for an open work environment. Designers were able to see what everyone was working on, and the exposed space generated more new ideas. We were the opposite of Marvin in this respect. Our new space was perfect for what we wanted to achieve. We bought new machinery and BMT was up and running one week after we closed MGA.

With only twenty-five employees, BMT was leaner and more cohesive than MGA.

Our new business grew and thrived. BMT kept turning out successful new toys and games, and we expanded our list of clients and continued to grow in output and income.

Rouben's office was next to mine in the new space. One day in the summer of 1988, Rouben walked in and set a book on my desk called *The Art of the Deal* by Donald Trump. Rouben, who concentrated primarily on dolls, thought there might be a game somewhere in the book and suggested I read it. Rouben said he had a connection to Donald Trump if I found anything worthwhile in his book.

Rouben's wife owned several stores in Water Tower Place in Chicago, including Benetton, Louis Vuitton, and Mount Blanc. Nina Terzian, a highly successful retailer, was an incredibly skilled merchandiser with a fabulous eye for detail. She was a tall, striking blonde—the opposite of Rouben's dark Armenian look. Nina had recently opened her first store in New York in Trump Tower. She believed she could arrange a meeting with Donald Trump if we had a board game to show him. She knew the manager of Trump's retail office and was confident she could make it happen. She was a force of nature, and what Nina wanted, Nina got.

Immediately, I started developing the Trump game. It obviously had to be a real estate game, but it needed to differ from Monopoly. The main features of the board game were properties: a casino, a condominium, a few office buildings, a golf resort, a shopping center, and even a theme park. The money denominations for the game were huge—$10 million to $500 million—befitting The Donald. I added his photograph to all the play money. I dreamed up a tag line for the game that I thought fit Trump perfectly: *It's Not Whether You Win or Lose, It's Whether You Win!* We created a beautiful prototype of a game box using Trump's photograph from the cover of his book. We called it Trump: The Game.

Nina Terzien's friend at Trump Tower arranged for Rouben and me to meet Trump on a Tuesday in the fall of 1988 in New York at the Tower.

As we were walking to our 2:00 p.m. meeting, I stopped at a Barnes & Noble on Fifth Avenue to pick up three copies of *The Art of the Deal*. Rouben asked me what I was doing with the books. I had an idea and told him, "You'll see."

We arrived at Trump's office at 1:50 p.m. and waited in the beautiful plush lobby of his office on Fifth Avenue. It dripped with Trump. The elevator opened and out walked The Donald. He was a big man, six feet, three inches tall, and the size of a pro football player. He just nodded to us and walked into his office. He had no idea who we were. I turned to Rouben and smiled, "At least they can't tell us he's not here."

At exactly 2:00 p.m., the receptionist announced, "Mr. Trump is ready for your meeting," and advised us that he was a mysophobe and didn't shake hands. She escorted us into his palatial corner office overlooking Central Park to the north. One entire wall must have had fifty framed magazine covers with his photograph. Trump opened immediately with, "Hello, let's see what you have." His lawyer was in the room and there was no small talk. I unwrapped our gorgeous game box and Trump smiled as he examined it. He specifically liked the tag line I had placed right under his name.

I opened up the game board, placed the property boxes on it, and showed him the huge-denomination bills with his picture on each one. He smiled again, but as I started to explain the rules, he cut me off with, "I like it. What's next?" He had no interest in playing the game. I said I was going to pitch it to my three largest clients and get back to him with a deal.

I quickly asked if he would do me a favor and he answered: "Sure, what?" "Would you please autograph three copies of your book, *The Art of the Deal*?" I told him the first one was to the president of Milton Bradley, the second to the president of Parker Brothers, and the third to Mattel's president. He smiled and said, "This is good." I took the autographed books, we said goodbye, and the meeting was over. It couldn't have lasted more than ten minutes.

The first call I made was to my good friend, Mel Taft, a senior VP at Milton Bradley. He flew to Chicago to see the game a few days later. Mel was excited about our prototype and Donald Trump, but surprised at the high cost of our financial proposal. Our normal royalty rate was 5 percent of the wholesale selling price. I asked for 12 percent on Trump: The Game. The advance against the royalty on a game like this without Trump or another character license might have been between $50,000 and $100,000. For the Trump Game, I asked for $500,000. Mel was overwhelmed by our request and told us he needed to talk with his bosses before agreeing to such a high rate. I told him to get back to me in a few days and promised I wouldn't show the game to anyone else until I heard back from him.

Mel called me the next day. "It's way too expensive, but we'll accept the terms because we don't want our competitors making it," he said. I made an appointment with Donald Trump and flew back to New York. He again was exactly on time for our appointment, which impressed me. This meeting was just the two of us in his office; not even his lawyer was present. I remember the exact conversation because of its brevity. "Hello, what's the deal?" he asked. There was no small talk about the flight or the family.

I first explained that our agreement was a big deal in the toy business (at that time). Perhaps it wasn't in the real estate business, but it was in the game business. Trump liked the percentage and advance number. Before he had a chance to say anything, I pointed to my chest and said "fifty" and pointed to him and said "fifty." "I don't do fifty/fifty," he replied. He pointed to his chest and said "sixty" and pointed to me and said "forty." I answered, "OK, we have a deal." We didn't shake hands.

He asked, "What else do I need to do?" I told him that the New York Toy Fair was in February and asked him to come to it in four months. I added that the games would be manufactured in East Longmeadow, Massachusetts, and said it would be great publicity if he could be there when the games were coming off the assembly line. He agreed to participate in both events, and he did.

When Milton Bradley introduced the game, the rules opened with Donald Trump's words:

> *Now that you are about to play my game, I invite you to live the fantasy! Feel the power! And make the deals!*

The object of the game is to make the most money. I'm talking about hundreds of millions of dollars. If you are clever, aggressive and lucky, you could end up with a billion or more!

...Play it smart and stack up huge profits! Pay too much and you could lose your shirt!

...Have fun—and remember, it's not whether you win or lose, but whether you win!

The next time I saw Donald Trump was at the New York Toy Fair in February. The game was a hit. I appreciated that Trump arrived at every meeting exactly on time and didn't squeeze me on the deal, which he could have. Trump could have proposed a 70/30 or even an 80/20 split—without Trump, we had no product, and he knew it. We had developed an excellent board game with some neat features, but it had no value without the Trump connection.

A decade later, we created the electronic, talking Apprentice Game. When I flew to New York, Trump liked the idea and approved the game. Trump recorded his lines, including his classic "You're fired," into a laptop computer that we brought to his conference room at Trump Tower. My experience working with Trump was as terrific as it had been ten years earlier. The Apprentice Game was not a success, however, probably because it was too expensive.

I was surprised when Donald Trump announced his candidacy for president in June 2015. I was shocked that this businessman and reality-show star was throwing his hat into the big political ring. I was also astonished as he methodically eliminated the other sixteen Republican candidates. When he got elected in November 2016, our country was surprised along with the rest of the world.

Chapter 20

Ellen DeGeneres Loves *Guesstures*

B ack in 1967, shortly after I started designing toys for MGA, Marlene and I invited five young married couples to our apartment for an evening of party games. I spread an assortment of Marvin Glass-designed games on the shag carpet in the living room (everyone had shag in the '60s). I briefly explained the rules of each game to everyone before we started playing, then we immediately started behaving like kids.

That night we played the classic Marvin Glass games from before my time, including Hands Down, Operation, Mouse Trap, and Rock 'Em Sock 'Em Robots. I included my new game, Bucket of Fun. My friends enjoyed sitting around on the floor and playing kid games. When I explained this was what I did at work, they were delighted. Like me, they were amazed that I got paid for playing with toys and games.

I always played along with my friends, quickly answering questions about rules and resolving any disputes. Like me, most of my friends were intensely competitive. I was attracted to serious game players who loved to win and, at least outwardly, were good losers. I brought in new games every time Marlene and I threw a party. We loved hosting game nights and carefully prepared for every gathering in our sparsely furnished apartment.

One evening, I decided we'd play charades, one of the great classic games, requiring only a pen, paper, and a willingness to appear completely silly and ridiculous as you gesture silently in front of your friends. Often, the sillier you act, the better. To prepare for the party, I wrote down movie titles, book titles, television shows, and familiar sayings on little pieces of paper. I couldn't play because I knew all the answers. But that night as I watched my friends play charades, they gave me an idea.

I wanted to create a new way to play charades. Players would still need to silently gesture to convey the written word, but I'd simplify the action and set a time limit to speed things up. I had to figure out how to design my updated version of charades so that we could license it to one of our clients. Then, I hoped, we'd collect lots of royalties. I wasn't sure at that moment how to develop my idea, but for twenty years it stayed in my mind, brewing and bubbling in the background.

My charades idea came to me in 1988, shortly after we closed MGA and opened BMT. Instead of players acting out movie and book titles, which were usually several words or a phrase, they would instead read just one word. They would act out nouns, verbs, or adjectives—any word that could be clearly conveyed, like "ballerina," "excited," or "frog." There would be three categories of words, rated easy, medium, and hard. Players would get more points for harder words. On every turn, each player would have to act out four words instead of one. I would invent a timer device and mechanism that would give them only seconds to get each of the four words right—or wrong. Eureka! I loved my concept, now I just needed to execute it.

What should I name it? I liked the idea of combining the words "guess" and "gestures" and came up with Guesstures, which is what I wrote when I pulled the job number and started working on my idea. Thinking up hundreds of words to write on playing cards was the easy part. The hard part was designing a new plastic mechanism that we could put in a plastic box to sell with the cards.

It took me a few weeks to create a working prototype of my mechanism. I built a plastic box that resembled a long, skinny blue toaster with a red timer button on the side. It had four consecutive slots on top, one slot for each of four cards. I created a deck of small two-by-three-inch cards. Each card had two words on one side. Easy words, worth one point, included ballerina, baby, and robot. Teacher, birthday, and firecracker were medium words worth two points. The hardest words, worth three points, included marathon, potato chip, and sunburn.

A player would place the cards into the slots, being sure that the words faced him or her and not their teammates. As soon as the player hit the red button, the machine started ticking and the pressure was on. The player had eight seconds to gesture each word to their team and grab the card before it disappeared into the "toaster." As soon as the card dropped away, or was saved for a score, you moved on to the next card. You had thirty-two seconds to correctly guess as many of the four words as possible.

We easily sold the game to the first person we pitched it to, Mel Taft at Milton Bradley. A significant advantage to selling Guesstures was that no batteries were required. Milton Bradley introduced the game in 1990, and they made several different television commercials to promote it. Guesstures was a big hit and is still selling today.

Inside the box, Milton Bradley's description of the game read:

> Act and guess as fast as you can in this hilarious, high-speed Guesstures game! All you have to do is pop four cards into the Action Timer, then set it and start acting fast! The words may look easy, but you only have a few seconds to use classic charades techniques to get your team to guess each one. Did your team guess right? Then you've got to grab the card out of the slot before it gets "munched" by the Action Timer! Easy cards are worth 1 point, Medium cards are worth 2, and Hard cards are worth 3. When the game's over, will your team have enough points to win?

BMT created an electronic version of Guesstures in 2005. It was a great design but a marketing disaster. We included thousands of words on a digital display but no cards. People missed playing in front of their friends, with the little cards dropping away into the slots and saving them for a score. The *tick...tick...tick...*was gone. All of the small elements that make the game fun to play with other people were missing. The electronic version was a flop, but the original game still sells well.

Years later, around 2010, one of the people at BMT told me Ellen Degeneres had played Guesstures on her daytime talk show. Wow! Fabulous! What a great promotion for my game. He described how Ellen had used a giant, five-foot-high stage replica of our game, including giant cards being munched by an Action Timer. One day I watched her play on her show and was delighted that she was clearly having so much fun with audience members and celebrities.

I called one of my contacts at Hasbro, which had bought out Milton Bradley years before and now owns the rights to Guesstures. My friend at Hasbro told me they were thrilled with the free publicity, but they had nothing to do with placing my game on her show. Hollywood is full of agencies that promote product placement in movies and television shows. If you're watching a show and someone is drinking a Pepsi or eating Reese's Pieces, those companies paid a lot of money for their products to be viewed.

Hasbro received incredible free promotion because Ellen Degeneres is a game nut and crazy about Guesstures. Moreover, she is a terrific player and an intense competitor. Some of the celebrities she's played Guesstures with on her show include Jimmy Fallon, Julia Roberts, Jennifer Garner, Collin Farrell, Christina Aguilera, and Adam Levine. There are dozens of YouTube videos showing Ellen energetically playing Guesstures with celebrities and studio audience guests.

Chapter 21

Building a Better Mouse Trap:
Hot Wheels, Barbie, and Polly Pocket

■ – – – – – – – – – – – – – ■

Marvin Glass & Associates and BMT prospered because we created unique and dynamic products that parents bought and children loved to play. Most of our concepts were original, appearing "out of thin air," or, more accurately, out of the vibrant imaginations of our employees. Some of our most lucrative creations, however, were modified additions to blockbuster toy brands invented and manufactured by our customers. Mattel, an important client and industry giant, manufactured three of our most profitable variations of Hot Wheels, Barbie, and the (financial) queen of them all, the diminutive Polly Pocket doll.

In 1945, three friends in a Los Angeles garage created what would grow to become one of the largest toy companies in the world, Mattel Inc. The husband-and-wife team of Elliot and Ruth Handler joined their friend Matt Matson to start Mattel Creations, taken from the two first names of Matt and Elliot. Elliot and Ruth soon bought out Matson due to his poor health.

Elliot Handler was a born tinkerer who had studied industrial design at the ArtCenter College of Design in Pasadena, California. He married Ruth in 1938, when they were both twenty-two years old, and in 1941, their daughter Barbie was born. Elliot worked producing objects such as picture frames, mirrors, and light fixtures. Elliot loved to experiment with plastic, particularly Lucite, and in the early 1940s he and Ruth started selling dollhouse furniture made out of plastic. Ruth wanted to try selling the merchandise and learned she was very good at it. Ruth suggested they concentrate on toys, and their first big hit was a plastic ukulele. They found the roles that they would play for the rest of their careers—Elliot was the designer and inventor, and Ruth was a shrewd and successful businesswoman.

Mattel invested heavily in television advertising and became the first major sponsor of *The Mickey Mouse Club* television show when it debuted in 1955. Just as Marvin Glass and Lionel Weintraub discovered when they advertised their products, Ruth and Elliot knew that advertising directly to children on television paid off. Remarkably, Ruth and Elliot each went on to develop products that stand as toy industry icons more than fifty years later. Ruth invented the Barbie doll and Elliot created Hot Wheels cars.

Ruth's idea for the Barbie doll was sparked when she observed her daughter Barbara playing with paper dolls for hours, pretending they were adults. At that time, dolls focused almost exclusively on younger girls who played with baby dolls they could mother. Dolls weren't marketed toward older girls. Ruth came up with the concept to create a plastic doll with an adult body, movable joints, and a cloth wardrobe. Like her daughter did with the paper dolls, older children could play with the plastic doll and imagine themselves living in an adult world.

Ruth had trouble convincing Elliot and other executives in the company that her Barbie doll would sell, but in 1956, she was traveling in Europe and saw the German-made Bild Lilli doll, which was an adult toy. The Bild Lilli doll was made of plastic, with articulated arms and legs, and Ruth saw that it was possible to manufacture the type of doll she had envisioned: a plastic, movable doll for older children. Ruth bought a Bild Lilli doll and took it back to show her designers in California. Soon, the Barbie doll was born.

When Barbie debuted at the New York Toy Fair in 1959, she didn't make a splash at first. But Ruth believed in her invention and decided to invest heavily in television advertising on *The Mickey Mouse Club*. The commercials paid off and Barbie soon rocketed Mattel and the Handlers to fame and fortune. Other dolls were added to Barbie's world, including a boy doll named after the Handlers' son, Ken. Today, Barbie is a global icon. More than one billion Barbie dolls in more than 150 countries have been sold.

Almost a decade after Barbie was introduced to the world, Elliot Handler invented his own blockbuster classic toy, Hot Wheels. Mattel introduced their first sixteen Hot Wheels cars in 1968. At the time, Tyco Toys had a conventional product called Matchbox cars on the market, and Elliot set out to eclipse Matchbox cars in every way. In 1953, Tyco had bought the rights to produce Matchbox cars from Lesney Products in the U.K.

Elliot wanted his cars to be hot rods and muscle cars that ignited a child's adrenaline. He used flaming paint jobs, superchargers, and over-sized rear tires to create an exciting performance car that, because of its wider wheels and heavier body, was the first toy car that would run on a track. Each car was manufactured from die-cast metal. The first car off the line was a dark blue custom Camaro. A plastic track was sold sepa-rately. Hot Wheels cars were a staggering success from day one.

In the mid-1970s, toy designers at Marvin Glass & Associates started tinkering with Hot Wheels ideas. They knew they couldn't improve on the car itself, but they wanted to improve on the fun factor. The goal was to get players to actively play with their cars, not just look at them. It wasn't long before they thought of a sure-fire way with a simple premise. What could be more fun than intentionally crashing little metal cars and trucks into each other? The more spectacular the crash, the better! You could send the cars flying off the track and through the air, spinning and smashing into the scenery below, narrating each crash as if it the cars were running in the Indy 500 or a NASCAR race.

As MGA's managing partner, I gave the project the green light to go ahead, although I can't remember which toy designer dreamed up the original idea. We created a simple design to guarantee fantastic results every time, no batteries required. Players assembled a banked, figure-eight racetrack out of blue plastic pieces. In the center of the figure-eight was a bright yellow reinforced intersection painted with the words "Criss Cross Crash." Players energized their metal cars by hand-cranking a wheel on the track that revved up an "engine" made of foam rollers that emitted a great whine. Every time the car raced around the track, it passed through the foam rollers, which gave it a power boost. The goal, as written on the back of the box, was to "Avoid the crash! Make it safely around the track!"

When we pitched the crashing car set to Mattel, they loved it. We introduced Criss Cross Crash in 1978, and it was a resounding hit. Later versions, introduced in 1994 and 2016, were motorized with batteries to make the cars go faster and eliminate hand-cranking. The set is still for sale today, more than forty years later. MGA continues to collect royalties on all of the Hot Wheels Criss Cross Crash designs.

MGA and Mattel enjoyed a productive relationship when I was hired in 1967, and it continued throughout my career. Mattel was one of our biggest clients and I knew several of the executives who worked there. In 1981, however, I met a woman at Mattel who would soon go on to become the brightest star in the toy industry: Jill Barad. Jill came from the cosmetics industry and had just turned thirty years old. I had no idea when I first met her that she would become the most brilliant toy executive in the world. After a year at Mattel, she was put in charge of the Barbie brand and grew it from $200 million in sales in 1982 to $1.9 billion in 1997. She became president and CEO of Mattel in 1992, when she was forty-one years old. At that time, you could count on one hand the number of female executives who were leading Fortune 500 companies.

When I met Jill, I had no idea how toy savvy she was. I only knew was that she was the most gorgeous woman I had ever met. She had long dark hair and was always dressed to kill. She could have been a Hollywood movie star, but she was in the toy business and an important client of Marvin Glass & Associates, which meant she was an important client of mine. She and I hit it off and became friends. Through the years Jill Barad and her movie-producer husband, Tom, became dear friends. I vacationed with them in Italy. I attended family bar mitzvahs and weddings. To this day she, Tom, and I are still friends.

Jill was one of the best marketing and merchandisers I've ever seen. She paid incredible attention to detail and knew how to present a great product—pricing, packaging, marketing, and merchandising. She used her knowledge of presentation from the cosmetics industry to great effect in the toy industry.

Jill and I remained lifelong friends because we kept our business and personal lives separate. Jill and I made a lot of deals through the years, and many people in the industry thought it was because Jill and I had a personal relationship. That just showed they didn't know Jill—with her, business was business. If we presented a new concept and she thought it was lousy, she said so, and we moved on. Clients weren't interested in making us feel good when they arrived at our office for a presentation. Clients were there to test what we had to sell. We had to have tough skin, because they said no a lot more than they said yes. Jill commonly turned us down, although she was the one who stepped in to see that Mattel paid us and gave us credit for one of our most profitable designs.

In 1991, one of our designers at BMT came up with an idea for Barbie that we thought must have been used before, but I still gave him the go-ahead to create his prototype invention. It occurred to us that since little girls loved to play with Barbie dolls, it should be possible to design a three-foot-tall Barbie who wears real clothes that a little girl could also wear. We thought someone on Mattel's Barbie design team must have already thought of this, but when we presented it to them at out office in Chicago, they were interested, although one of the executives said that their own in-house toy designers had already been working on a similar idea and they wouldn't pay us for it. However, when Jill Barad reviewed our idea, she recognized that our idea was nothing like what her team was working on, and she ordered that BMT be paid and given credit for the invention.

In 1992, the My Size Barbie debuted. She stood thirty-eight inches tall and had long, blonde wavy hair. She came with two party outfits. One was a gown with a silver beaded top, pink frilly skirt with a bow, and pink shoes. She even wore a silver tiara. The other was a lavender top with a different pink skirt and a pink tiara. The pieces could mix-and-match for children to make up their own outfits. Some three- or four-year-old girls could wear My Size Barbie's clothes.

My Size Barbie was a hit, so two years later we designed and Mattel manufactured My Size Bride Barbie. This Barbie had wide blue eyes and long, straight blonde hair and wore a glamorous white gown and a sparkling necklace with a bright blue jewel. The box advertised, "Wear & share Barbie doll's bridal gown!" Girls all over the world did.

In 1996, we ushered in our last iteration on the theme, the Dancing My Size Barbie. She was a blue-eyed, blonde-haired dancer wearing a full-length dancing gown in sky blue and white. She stood on a special dance stand and kids could send her twirling and gliding across the floor. All three of our Barbie doll designs sold well and further cemented our great working relationship with Mattel, the biggest toy company in the world, who would soon go on to manufacture our highest grossing toy ever—by far.

I never saw it coming.

Our most profitable toy to date, for both MGA and BMT, was a tiny doll that was, coincidentally, manufactured by a British friend of mine, Sir Torquil Norman. I met Torquil in the early 1980s at the British Toy Fair in London and we instantly hit it off. He stood six-foot-seven with sandy hair, a genial smile, and twinkling eyes. Torquil was a former RAF fighter pilot whose father helped organize British paratroopers in World War II and was killed in action.

Torquil was an accidental toy merchant—a British-born, Harvard-educated businessman and banker who turned his hand to toys to try to save a failing company. In 1980, when he was forty-seven years old, Torquil founded his company, Bluebird Toys, in the bucolic town of Swindon, England, about seventy miles west of London. Bluebird Toys stayed in business but didn't make it big until 1989, when they introduced a toy supernova to the world, the Polly Pocket doll.

Polly was a tiny doll, less than one inch high, who lived inside a miniature playset tucked inside a folding compact case. When a child opened the case, they saw a blonde-haired girl in a bright red sleeveless shirt, red headband, and red shoes. Her circular base was designed to fit snugly inside tiny holes in the case so she could stand up and move about her intricately designed and furnished apartment. The dolls had adjustable arms and legs and bent at the waist to fit inside the folding compact case when it was closed.

Sales were sensational, and new variations of Polly Pocket dolls were introduced annually. In its second year, 1990, Polly's Beach House came in a soft green compact that could fit easily inside a bag or purse. There were two adjustable dolls, Polly Pocket, with blonde curls and a red headband, and a blonde-haired boy, Wee Willie, dressed in a yellow T-shirt and blue pants. When a child opened the compact, the upper half included two bedrooms, a bath and an eating area, and the lower half displayed a pond with a dock and pier. Crucially, the gate to the dock opened, and later Polly Pockets increased the number of moving parts in the cases, including spinning carousels and spinning rockets. New characters were invented. The tiny rooms displayed incredible details and colors, including beds, pillows, dressers, tables, clocks, and windows.

Mattel held the distribution arrangement with Bluebird Toys in the 1990s, and when their business slowed in 1998, Bluebird Toys became the target of multiple hostile takeovers. Fortunately for us, Mattel finally bought out Bluebird later that year, and soon redesigned Polly before putting her back on the market. Mattel made Polly slightly bigger, at just under four inches tall, and gave her a more lifelike appearance. Polly also now wore a straight ponytail instead of a bob.

Polly Pocket miniature dolls were wildly popular despite the problems of manufacturing their tiny cloth clothes. It was also difficult for little girl's hands to dress the dolls. One of our designers at BMT, Robert Annis, was looking at Polly Pocket when he had a fabulous idea. Why not make it easier for little girls to dress their dolls by using a new type of material for the doll clothes?

He created clothes out of a new type of soft, plastic material made of vinyl and silicone. The new material made it much easier for small hands to dress and undress the tiny dolls. It was also easier for manufacturers to make tiny clothes out of soft plastic than cloth fabric. "Polly Stretch" fabric was invented, and the new Fashion Polly doll was born. To my amazement, Fashion Polly Pocket was the most profitable toy in either MGA's or BMT's history. Sales dwarfed those of every other product we ever produced, including Simon, Operation, and Rock 'Em Sock 'Em Robots. We couldn't believe it when we saw the royalty statements that arrived every quarter.

When Torquil Norman was later interviewed on television about producing Polly Pocket, he said, "It was such fun and so easy to think of new things to do with her." He added, "We had so many options as to what to make. Eventually we made little houses where you lift the roof off and every house had a bulb and a battery so it lit up, so when you put Polly to bed and shut the roof the windows lit up."

When asked to explain his success, Torquil replied, "I really liked the toy industry, and I had a homemade research team with five young children. It worked out very well." He described the two qualifications he believed were needed for making toys. "First, an eye for detail, because young people are very interested in small details," he smiled, adding, "second, a mental age of about seven.... I qualified very well, because I never really grew up inside as far as toys were concerned."

Torquil, whose unusual name was Scottish, loved to say, "I don't want to rearrange the deck chairs, I want to redesign the ship." One year he did exactly that. Torquil bought a steel-hulled river barge, gutted it and rebuilt it with three staterooms, including a master bedroom with a seven-foot bed and two smaller suites. Torquil let me borrow his fabulous rebuilt barge one summer in the late 1980s. I invited two couples for a one-week journey down the Burgundy Canal in France—Howard and Pauline, and my brother Gene and his wife Gillian. We drew straws for the master suite with the seven-foot bed. Howard, the shortest man among us, won. We hired Torquil's captain and his wife to steer us through the spectacular French countryside while we sipped fabulous wines and enjoyed *la bonne vie.*

After Torquil left the toy industry in 1998, he put together an investment group and bought an old iron locomotive switching station in the heart of London. He developed the Camden Roundhouse into an art, theater, and music school designed to provide increased opportunities to disadvantaged British youngsters. Years later, in recognition of his remarkable service to the arts and to youth, Queen Elizabeth II knighted Torquil Norman.

Our Hot Wheels, Barbie, and Polly Pocket variations were based on existing toys, but our unique ideas belonged to us. As always, it was our employees, friends, and good connections within the toy industry that made it possible for us to prosper. We invented wonderful products, but like any creative endeavor, much of our work was centered on the importance of human relations.

Chapter 22

Finding New Blood and the Hall of Fame

H iring new talent is the lifeblood of every enduring company. My partners and I were constantly on the lookout for new designers, searching for people with the elusive ability to both feel like a child and translate those feelings into a lucrative toy or game. I often traveled to speak to and recruit young talent.

I focused on the Fashion Institute of Technology in New York City, which had an excellent two-year post-graduate program in toy design. I traveled to the Otis College of Art and Design in Los Angeles, which offered a four-year undergraduate degree in toy design. It was the only such program in the country. Their graduates were terrific toy designers, and we hired several of them. We were always cautious about students who grew up in Los Angeles and moved to Chicago to work for us. They often hightailed it back to California after one snowy Chicago winter. I also visited the industrial design departments at the Cleveland Institute of Art, Carnegie Mellon University, Ohio State University, and my alma mater, the University of Illinois.

We hired designers and engineers who appeared promising, but we could rarely be sure of those new employees ahead of time, and most of them failed as toy inventors. There were a few times, however, when, like toys, I was immediately sure we'd hit a home run.

One of those times was when we hired a young man from Ed Zagorski's industrial design program at the University of Illinois.

In 1979, Ed called to tell me about a remarkably talented student of his who was about to graduate, Don Rosenwinkel. I told Ed to send him to me. I met Rosenwinkel, looked over his portfolio, and hired him on the spot, much like Marvin Glass had done with me twelve years earlier. Don turned out to be a grand slam.

The best new employee for any creative company is someone who brings a fresh vision. If you only train someone for a particular job, and never get someone who constantly surprises, you've just maintained the status quo. Don was that fresh talent for us—he was our next boy genius (Marvin's words). My life was shaped by three mentors: Hazel Loew, Ed Zagorski, and Marvin Glass. You have to go out and get people to mentor you—they don't just come to you. I had reached out three times, and now I was ready to be a mentor myself.

Don hit the ground running. He was creative and incredibly productive with a natural instinct for toys and games. Like many other successful toy designers, Don had invented toys and other mechanical objects as a young boy with his dad. He was a great engineer and mechanic and built terrific prototypes. I often asked for his advice when I wasn't able to solve a problem. I watched Don grow and mature, although not too much; he remained a child at heart, like all great toy designers.

A decade later, in 1988, when Howard, Rouben, and I started our own toy company, Breslow, Morrison & Terzian, (BMT), we made Don Rosenwinkel and another toy designer, John Zaruba, junior partners. We groomed them to take over when we retired. Don and I were friends as well as coworkers. He was six feet tall, a handsome, slender man with dark hair who had married a fellow University of Illinois industrial design graduate. Karen was incredibly talented and went to work for Braun Company in Chicago creating cosmetic bottles. Don and Karen raised three creative, talented daughters. Their girls were ten years younger than my three sons, but we shared the collective accomplishments of our children as they grew up.

In 1992, Mattel bought the rights to manufacture Uno, an interactive card game for children and adults with numbers, colors and actions that require a player to shout out "Uno!" when they have one card remaining. In essence, Uno was a knockoff of Crazy Eights. Mattel promoted Uno into a fabulous worldwide success, and there were soon variations on the market such as Uno Bingo, Uno Junior, and Uno Hearts.

In the mid-1990s, Uno caught Don Rosenwinkel's imagination. He had an idea for an electronic version of the card game that would rachet up its speed, unpredictability, and excitement. As toy designers, we were always looking at how to build new devices in ways that children had fun interacting with. You didn't succeed as a toy designer unless you knew how to build things. Designers always make mistakes as they're inventing, but the missteps are either fixed or the game isn't made.

Using foam rollers, Don built a mechanical device he called the Uno Attack Launcher. It housed the cards and sent them flying out of the machine in random numbers when a player pushed the "launch" button. The launcher used three C batteries and was bright red with bold yellow letters spelling "UNO" along the side. The finished product looked something like an oversize, rounded stapler. Don designed the launcher so that it "attacked" the player—to win the game you had to be the first to get rid of all of your cards.

In 1998, Mattel introduced Uno Attack. It became a huge success and was one of the top income earners for BMT. The Uno Attack box shows an animated, smiling family of four with their hands on the cards around a table, and reads, "UNPREDICTABLE EXCITEMENT Every Time You Press The Draw Button!"

I was proud of Don's fabulous success and happy that his career had blossomed. I had learned from Marvin Glass that it was important to take care of our employees and clients as well as our friends and families. In the end, Marvin's greatest genius lay in his ability to motivate people. I didn't share Marvin's gift—no one did—but years before, not long after taking over as managing partner at MGA, I started reminding people that I was thinking of them on their special day. I was blessed with a happy home life and a great career, and I wanted to share my happiness with others. In keeping with my fun occupation, I decided to have fun with my friends and family.

In the fall of 1980, I was in a liquor store looking for a birthday gift, a bottle of champagne. I saw a display of Moet & Chandon with several different-size bottles. I knew a standard bottle contained about six glasses of bubbly. The store displayed everything from a gigantic Rehoboam, which holds six standard bottles, to a diminutive Piccolo, which holds a quarter of a bottle. Standing there, looking at the champagne bottles, I got an idea that I went on to celebrate for the next twenty-five years. I started a birthday club.

I decided I would send a Piccolo bottle of Moet & Chandon as a birthday present to family, friends, partners, and special clients. The small bottle contained two glasses of Champagne and would be fun—more than a Hallmark card but not extravagant. In order to make my gift unique, I designed my own pressure-sensitive label to stick over the Moet label. I personalized the label with the message, "Cheers on Your Birthday!"

I planned to send out gifts of these cute little bottles every month. I decided to call it "The Brez Birthday Club." (My nickname has always been Brez. Somehow the "S" in my last name became more of a "Z" sound and my new name stuck. Many friends still call me Brez, and grown children of my friends still call me Mr. Brez.)

I made a list of all of the birthdays I knew and put them on a new calendar for 1981. There were about fifty birthdays when I was done. I was missing birthdays of lots of people I wanted in my club, so I started casually asking them questions. I had a guise that I often used: "I heard on the radio that today is Marilyn Monroe's birthday—hey, when is yours?" Lots of people thought I was some kind of astrology nut.

I bought fifty bottles of Moet Piccolos, getting a good price for them. I bought long, small boxes that fit the Piccolo by adding a little bubble wrap. I enlisted my oldest son, Marc, who was ten, my middle son, Michael, who was seven, and my smallest guy, Joey, who was only three. Joey helped as much as he could on the family project. We bubble-wrapped all the bottles and taped up the boxes. Everything was ready. I calculated the postage and made mailing labels. I mailed out a few gift bottles in the last week of December 1980, headed to the members whose birthdays fell in early January. The Brez Birthday Club was launched!

I received many calls and written notes of thanks in the club's inaugural year. I enjoyed the happy process of remembering birthdays with a special gift. By the summer, I started working on my idea for the second year. I found a cute little square glass jar, filled it with pistachio nuts and sent it out with a silly note for 1982.

The club kept growing, and in the third year I gave a full-size, multicolored beach towel. I drew cartoons of people using the towel for different purposes and wrote a birthday note which read,

A towel is a very versatile birthday gift.
You can sun yourself on a Caribbean beach,
you can cry about your age and dry your eyes,
you can take that special birthday bath,
you can cut it into rags and wash your car,
however you use it, have a very nice day, Jeffrey Breslow

My dad made the towels and gave me a good price, although they were still the most expensive present I ever sent. The beach towel was one of my all-time favorites. Years later, I saw a young girl on Oak Street Beach sunning herself on my birthday towel. I introduced myself and showed her my name on her towel. At first she thought I was a weirdo. Her father was in my club, and somehow she had ended up with my towel.

One time, I got a call from a good client who was divorced and estranged from his grown children. In a choked-up voice he told me that aside from his mother, I was the only person who remembered his birthday. I never imagined my little gift would affect people so strongly, and I was very touched by his words.

Through the years I delivered books, T-shirts, picture frames, playing cards, bubble bath, honey, maple syrup, soap in the shape of a rubber duck, caramel corn, memo note pads, a coffee cup with everyone's name printed on it, candles, and other gifts. Dreaming up the personalized birthday presents each year was great fun, and I never ran out of ideas.

After a quarter of a century, I ended the club in 2005 with my final gift. I bought 540 little square books, each containing 365 pages. I created the outside cover of the book and wrote, "The Hidden Meaning of Birthdays." On the inside flap I wrote:

> *After 25 years, it is time to bid farewell to the Brez Birthday Club with this final gift. The club was started in 1981 with about 50 members, all of whom were sent a small split of Champagne. Today, the membership list stands at 540 worldwide. It has been a true delight keeping in touch with so many wonderful people over all these years. I will miss it and wish each of you many, many happy and healthy birthdays in the years to come. It has been a pleasure to have you as a member of the Brez Birthday Club. Love, Brez.*

When I was a kid, my dad taught me that giving was always better than receiving. I didn't understand that idea when I was ten years old. It took many years and my birthday club to help me understand my dad's words of wisdom. Just perhaps, if today is your special day,

A VERY HAPPY BREZ BIRTHDAY TO YOU!

My enjoyment of people extended to meeting new clients and seeing old friends at the annual New York Toy Fair every February. The last

Saturday of the trade show meant the toy fair dinner, a black-tie fund-raiser for charitable causes held in the grand ballroom of a fancy New York hotel. It was attended by four hundred or five hundred members of the industry, including all the who's who.

In 1985, the Toy Manufacturers of America (TMA) created the Toy Industry Hall of Fame to honor people who had made a significant contribution to the trade. It was a big deal when I went to my first awards ceremony that year. I continued to attend the event every year for the next twenty-three years until I retired from the toy business. I went through three different tuxedoes.

When they started choosing the men and women to honor, the most important criterion was the individual's contribution to the toy industry. There was always a slate of names that the member companies voted on. The names of the people inducted were publicly known in advance of the dinner, so the award wasn't a surprise.

One last requirement to win a place in the Hall of Fame was that you had to be *dead*. What a stupid idea for the toy business. In the first year, Marvin Glass was among the people inducted, along with Louis Marx and Merrill Hassenfeld. However, after about seven years of only honoring dead people, things were about to change.

I was a board member of the TMA (now the Toy Association) when Bernie Loomis came up with a brilliant idea. Bernie, the president of Kenner Products, was also the president of the awards committee and a brilliant marketer and toy expert. He knew potential when he came upon it: he saw enormous promise in the *Star Wars* movies becoming a line of toys for Kenner, and sure enough, it was a GIGANTIC HIT. So when Bernie suggested at one of our board meetings that it would be wonderful if we started honoring people while they were still alive, it was sure to be a great idea—and it was. I also think we were running out of dead people.

Everyone agreed with Bernie's idea, and he was the first living inductee into the Hall of Fame in 1992. Bernie enjoyed the honor for fourteen years until he died of heart failure in 2006. Bernie Loomis was an excellent client and friend and one of many brilliant people who helped build the toy industry and bring great joy to many children all around the world.

In 1996, Dick Grey, the president of Tyco Toys, was the award winner. He was a client of BMT, a friend, and a brilliant toy man. Howard, Rouben, and I were asked to present the Hall of Fame Award to Dick at the black-tie dinner.

Years before Dick was inducted, BMT had designed a toy for Tyco called the Magic Potty Baby doll. It wasn't a big success. It was a soft-body non-mechanical doll that came with a magic potty. The potty had a plastic toilet seat on which the child placed the baby. The sides of the potty were two plastic tubes, one inside the other. There was a very narrow gap between the two. The outside tube was clear plastic, and the inside tube was opaque white. When you sat the baby on the potty, a mechanism released yellow water that started to fill the narrow space between the two tubes from the bottom up. It was a closed system with very little yellow water. It was magic.

When the baby was done peeing, you flushed the toilet, the yellow water disappeared, and you could make the baby pee over and over again. Many people who bought this doll for their young daughters thought it was a great device for potty training a little girl. It was!

Jump back to 1996 and Dick Grey's induction. Unbeknownst to him, we had made a giant four-foot-tall replica of the Magic Potty that worked just like the toy potty. We built it in our toy studio in Chicago and had it shipped to the hotel in New York to be ready for the awards dinner. We hid it behind the curtain to surprise Dick just before we gave him the award. One small problem: we needed an adult to sit on the giant potty to complete the illusion and make the prop effective. It wouldn't be as much fun unless someone took a "seat."

When the awards night arrived, the three of us took the stage and talked about Dick Grey and his accomplishments—and, of course, spoke about the Magic Potty Doll that we had licensed to his company. I think I must have lost the coin flip with Howard and Rouben, because I was the one who took a seated pee in front of five hundred people. The curtain opened to roars from all the attendees, I took off my tuxedo jacket (but kept my pants on) and climbed up on the giant potty. I sat down and the potty started to fill with yellow pee. We brought the house down.

Two years later, in 1998, Howard Morrison, Rouben Terzian, and I were inducted into the Hall of Fame. The three of us were honored at the annual black-tie dinner in New York City. That's when I bought my third tuxedo, which is now in my closet and still fits.

The honorees always had a presenter who said a few words on their behalf, then the honoree would come on stage to receive their award. Jill Barad, the president of Mattel Toys and a great friend, spoke for me and presented me with the award. Jill's wonderful speech was beyond touching and was my true award.

I was delighted to have my family and friends with me that night. Years earlier, however, as my sons were growing into their teens, I realized that my wife Marlene and I had grown apart. In the mid-1980s, I'd found a new passion in adventure travel, which Marlene wanted no part of. We had divorced in the summer of 1996, but I was fortunate to have many people join me on my big night.

The Toy Manufacturers Association created a large aluminum plaque, two feet by four feet, and displayed it in the building where the annual toy fair was held in New York City. Howard, Rouben, and I have our names inscribed on that aluminum plaque, and we made a duplicate, which is mounted on the wall at the BMT toy studio in Chicago. The award allowed us to be in the company of the seventy-one individuals who had already earned their place in the Hall of Fame. Most important, I had the pleasure of knowing and working with most of these people during my forty-one years in the profession. Many of them built the business while I was still a child playing with toys.

The award was certainly an honor, but the best honor is having spent more than half my life in an industry that allowed me to celebrate the child within me all of my life. It allowed me to design products that brought joy and entertainment to millions and millions of young people all around the world. And after many years of toil and effort, it provided me with the means to explore my own personal adventures with family and friends.

Chapter 23

Adventures

In 1953, when I was ten years old, my parents drove Gene and me in a 1953 Oldsmobile sedan to California and back along historic Route 66. This was three years before the Eisenhower Interstate Highway System was even authorized. We were on the road for several weeks, and it was a long journey but still a great family adventure. On the way west, we stopped at the highlight of our trip—Arizona's Grand Canyon.

I was awestruck by the vistas from the South Rim of the magnificent canyon. Like most tourists, I walked only a few hundred yards down the Bright Angel Trail before turning around, but I found the sight mesmerizing. We spent one night there, but before we left, my dad bought me a View-Master stereoscopic viewer with twenty-one photos of the depths of the Grand Canyon. The View-Master, invented in 1939, had a slot for a circular cardboard disc that held fourteen small slides. When the user looked through the View-Master, a three-dimensional color photograph burst into life in front of their eyes. I spent hours soaking in the spectacular views of the steep, immense, colorful canyon.

Over the years my dad bought me View-Master discs of all the places we traveled, including Carlsbad Caverns and New York. With my eyes up to my viewer, I relived our journeys and dreamed of other places I hoped to visit one day, but nothing grabbed my imagination like the Grand Canyon. I bought books, maps, and photos to keep my dreams of another visit alive, but school, jobs, marriage, and family always came first. It wasn't until thirty-three years after my first visit that I finally made a return trip to the Grand Canyon.

In 1986, I took my first rafting trip through the Grand Canyon with a friend. I had learned during my years of study that the best way to experience the canyon was to take a rafting trip down the mighty Colorado River, which snaked its way through the valley a mile down from the rim. The idea of sleeping on the sandy beaches of the Colorado with the glow of the stars and moon overhead was impossible to resist any longer.

I had envisioned shooting the whitewater rapids many times, but the reality was even more exhilarating than I imagined. The feel of the frigid water on my skin, the roaring sounds of the rushing river, and the bouncing and bucking of the raft sent my adrenaline into overdrive. We sliced past giant boulders and flashed through smaller rock formations, all the while conscious of the foaming spray and swirling currents that shot us through the water. Our guide was masterful. When we emerged into the quiet flow after the rapids, we were elated. Our wet clothes and skin dried quickly in the baking desert sun.

All of the guides were geologists, and as we floated through calm water, we learned in detail about the rock formations and the hundreds of millions of years it took to create this marvel. We hiked through side canyons where we saw big horned sheep and discovered spectacular hidden waterfalls. We enjoyed great food and relaxed in the evenings. We didn't wear watches and had no connection with the outside world, which was rejuvenating. It gave me time to think and relax. We got up with the sun and dozed off in the dark.

This trip marked a turning point in my life. I decided it was time to enjoy similar experiences with more friends and family. I had worked hard and been successful, and after our trip, I started another club—the

Brez Adventure Club. I called the rafting company and reserved an entire trip for sixteen passengers for 1988, two years away. I booked the trip for the first week of June, which promised the best weather. Most people don't plan so far in advance, so I waited until the fall of '87 to start talking up the trip with friends. Marlene wasn't an outdoor person and wasn't interested in adventure travel, so this was going to be an all-guys trip. In 1988, fifteen guys and I rafted down the Colorado River for the first trip of the Brez Adventure club.

In 1991, my three boys were seventeen, fourteen, and nine, and I wanted to enjoy more time with my children in the outdoors. For me, there was only one place to take my boys—the Grand Canyon, the lady of my dreams. Sadly, Joey was too young to come on the first trip. I have returned to the Grand Canyon eight times since that memorable trip with my boys. I've rafted down the Colorado with my sons three times, as well as with other family and friends. I have rafted other whitewater, including rivers in California, Alaska, Idaho, and Wisconsin, and the Futaleufu in Chile. They were all spectacular experiences, but only the Grand Canyon refuses to release her hold on me.

I've skied in Idaho, Wyoming, Utah, Vermont, Canada, and Europe. Friends often ask, "What is your favorite place to ski?" My answer is always the same: "If the sun is shining, the snow is deep and powdery, and the weather is in the twenties, that's my favorite place to ski." On my bucket list is a summer ski trip to Chile or New Zealand with my brother Gene. I no longer ski bumps or black diamond runs. I'm just happy cruising the blue runs. As I get older, the après-skiing just keeps getting better.

I also trekked throughout Europe, including one arduous journey along the Way of St. James, a famous pilgrimage route that winds for about five hundred miles through the mountains of France and Spain. The trek lasted thirty-three days, and during those days I spoke English to people from twenty-eight countries. In New Zealand, I hiked with a guide who took us off the beaten paths and then drank wine at the end of each day's exertions. In the Kingdom of Bhutan, in South Asia, I faced treacherous mountain paths and raging rivers, but I loved the spectacular, peaceful country. I was a confident horseback rider and took challenging riding trips in Africa, India, Peru, and India, as well as ten summers riding the western Wyoming.

The Brez Adventure Club started in 1988. I decided to make it co-ed so that wives and girlfriends could join us. Some of the guys were annoyed, but they accepted it. We went hiking in Bryce and Zion canyons in Utah. For mysterious beauty, nothing can rival the hoodoos of Bryce Canyon. Hoodoos are tall, slender spires of rock that arise from the bottom of dry basins. The red, orange, and white colors of the sedimentary rock appear as if they were carved by drunken giants. Photographs can't do these remarkable shapes justice—nothing can match seeing the hoodoos in person. I've enjoyed many adventures with friends and family through the years, but none of my stories can compare to the incredible adventure endured by a friend I made at a gathering of toy makers.

All of my clients were members of our trade organization, the Toy Manufacturers of America. As toy designers only, Marvin Glass & Associates was the first non-manufacturing company invited to join the TMA. Our annual meetings were held in May at fun, warm places. The Boca Raton Hotel in Florida and Phoenician Hotel in Scottsdale, Arizona, were two of the favorites. In the afternoons we could sit by the pool or compete in serious tennis or golf matches. Spouses were always invited, and every Saturday night there was a gala black-tie dinner. The meetings were great fun and I never missed one.

While we played in the afternoons and evenings, we worked in the mornings. There were panel discussions by members and updates on government regulations affecting the toy industry. I even got to speak once about designing toys, and it was a terrific experience.

The annual meetings ended with a high-powered motivational speaker, and they were always thrilling and usually the best part of the program. In 2001, however, the keynote speaker was more than just inspirational—he became my most extraordinary friend, Nando Parrado.

Nando is now well known through the movie and book *Alive: The Story of the Andes Survivors* by Piers Paul Read. Read's book is a riveting account of a team of teenage rugby players from Uruguay whose plane crashed at twelve-thousand feet in 1972 in the snow-capped Andes mountains in Argentina. Of the forty-five passengers and crew on the plane, sixteen miraculously survived for seventy-two days. The survivors watched their friends and family members die of their injuries, exposure, and starvation as they endured bitter cold while waiting for a rescue plane that never came.

It was Nando Parrado and his friend Roberto Canessa who hiked for eleven days through the mountains heading west toward Chile. Near death, they found a farmer on horseback who led them to civilization. Nando flew in one of the rescue helicopters to direct the pilots to the plane's broken fuselage. Without his guidance, the remaining fourteen survivors would surely have perished.

Nando's speech to us at the toy association meeting was about survival under the most difficult, horrible conditions imaginable. He spoke about what it took to survive his ordeal. He wanted us to understand that people don't know what they are capable of until they are confronted with such an extreme situation. Nando's talk was the most powerful and stimulating story I had ever heard.

That Saturday night, we celebrated the end of the meeting with a barbecue instead of a fancy dinner dance. Nando attended the event, and many of us asked him questions, which he graciously answered. I hung around him all evening to learn more about him. I had never met a real live hero who, because of his incredible will and desire to live, had saved his own life and those of fifteen other boys. I have been fortunate to spend many hours with him since then.

In 2006, thirty-four years after the crash, Nando published his own story of the disaster, *Miracle in the Andes*. When Nando came to downtown Chicago during his book tour, I met him at the Barnes & Noble bookstore and gave him a big hug. I bought thirty-five copies of his book and lugged them in a taxi back to my toy studio, Big Monster Toys. Later that day, Nando came to BMT and gave a shortened version of his speech to the studio employees and autographed a book for each person there, giving us all a memorable day.

I saw him again in 2015 when Nando was speaking at the Lake Tahoe Shakespeare Festival on the shore of the lake. That morning I had breakfast with him, my brother Gene, and some other friends. Nando told us he could speak every day of the week if he wanted to, but he limits himself to a few speeches a month. He has a life back in Montevideo, Uruguay, with his wife, Veronique, and their two grown daughters, Veronica and Cecilia.

In 2019, my brother Gene and I took a trip to South America. We hiked in the spectacular Patagonia region of southern Chile and then traveled to Buenos Aires, which we loved. Our final stop was in Uruguay, specifically to see Nando in his own country. We went to Punta del Este, where Nando picked us up at our hotel and drove us to his home on the ocean to meet his wife, Veronique. We headed to lunch at La Huella, a beautiful restaurant on the beach where a table for Nando was waiting. Forty-seven years after the plane crash, he is still a revered celebrity in his country. At lunch I asked Nando if there was a monument to the crash survivors and the people who died. When he said there was not, an idea for a sculpture came to me instantly.

I drew a sketch of a giant boulder with sixteen stones the size of rugby balls attached to the top of it. These stones represent the survivors. There are also twenty-nine slender steel rods drilled into the top of the boulder that stand twelve feet tall. On top of each of these rods is a fist-sized stone representing one of the twenty-nine people who died. The twenty-nine stones atop the rods sway in the breeze. The sculpture took eighteen months to complete.

I shipped the five-ton sculpture, *Milagro en los Andes* (*Miracle in the Andes*), to Uruguay, where it stands on the grounds of Museo de Arte Contemporáneo Atchugarry in Punta del Este. The dedication will take place October 13, 2022, the fiftieth anniversary of the airplane crash. I have met lots of amazing people in my life, but none as courageous and spectacular as Nando Parrado.

Chapter 24

Creativity Is a Function of Pressure

Howard Morrison, Rouben Terzian, and I led charmed careers. We always made money and we always had fun. We never fought—ever. Because we were toy designers, we also never really grew up. We acquired wisdom but never lost the child residing inside of us. The three of us played in the sandbox together until we each left the toy business when we turned sixty-five.

In 1997, the year before the three of us were inducted into the Toy Industry Hall of Fame, Howard Morrison had retired. Our partnership agreement at BMT was different than the agreement at Marvin Glass—we arranged it so that retiring partners wouldn't cripple the long-term economic health of the company. A retired partner would continue to receive his full income for the next five years. He would also receive income on all new products. After five years, his income ceased and his ownership percentage was divided among the remaining active partners. This worked for both the individual and the future of the business.

Rouben Terzian was next to retire, when he turned sixty-five in 2001, leaving me as the sole original partner. Don Rosenwinkel and John Zaruba were now full partners at BMT. We were aware that the fifteen-year lease on our studio was going to run out in 2003, and Don, John, and I thought we should buy our own studio. Don found a great space at a large, sixty-year-old trucking garage in the West Loop, a few blocks from Oprah Winfrey's Harpo studio. The neighborhood was starting to gentrify, and we bought the empty garage at 21 S. Racine Avenue.

We now owned 18,000 square feet on ground level, complete with indoor parking. We worked with the architecture firm Pappageorge Hames to create our toy design studio and turn it into a showplace. We added skylights down the center of the building and installed a toy electric train around the ceiling. Each employee was given a train car that they were allowed to design in any way they wanted—one employee made their car into a shrine to the Chicago Bulls, and I made a little wooden sculpture for my car. The ceiling was so high that we had a life-size plush giraffe in the middle of the design area and a stuffed gorilla swinging on a large rope from the ceiling. The large overhead-door truck entrance was artfully painted to appear like a giant cartoon-style door with an enormous doorknob—and a bright green scowling monster with bulging white eyes and a toothy grimace who glares out the window at potential customers.

We also decided to change the company name when we moved to our new studio in 2003. We wanted to create a fun name out of the acronym BMT, and we came up with one we all loved—Big Monster Toys. The image of the giant green grimacing monster looking out the window of the garage door, created by Dino Crisanti, became our new logo and mascot. I spent five fabulous years at our new studio before it was my turn to hand over the reins.

I knew I would be leaving the toy business on June 5, 2008, when I turned sixty-five. I was looking forward to being able to devote all my time to my own interests. As I spent more time outdoors, both in Vermont and on my adventure travels, I found joy and inspiration in the incredible beauty around me. I felt galvanized to pursue one of my first great passions, sculpting.

I had created my first sculpture in Hazel Loew's high school art class when I was sixteen years old. I carved a semi-abstract, nude female form out of hard mahogany wood. After more than six decades, she still sits on my desk next to my computer. I call her *Hazel.*

At the University of Illinois, I had studied sculpture with the famous and brilliant sculptor Frank Gallo. To his credit, Gallo was a great teacher in addition to being a gifted sculptor, which is a rare combination. When I finished his class, however, I didn't sculpt again for more than forty years. During that time, my life was happily filled with designing toys, raising my sons, and adventure travels. I was too busy to notice that part of me missed the artistic act of sculpting. I had surrounded myself with beautiful art and sculpture, and as my retirement beckoned, I realized I wanted to devote my time to sculpting.

I started sculpting again in 2004. I wanted to turn my hand to sculpting again before I fully left the toy business. With my adventures in mind, I decided to construct a life-size bronze sculpture of myself hiking with a backpack, boots, and wooden pole. Working in an out-of-the-way spot in the studio, I fashioned a full-size framework out of iron wire. I sprayed the wire body with pink foam that solidified, then sculpted the structure and covered it with a skin of clay. I worked on it in the evenings and on weekends for three months before I was happy with my result. I sent the piece to the Illinois Art Casting Foundry to be cast in bronze, then shipped the finished product to Vermont, where I had a second home.

Inspired by Vermont and my active life outdoors, I soon sculpted a life-size horse in memory of my mom, who had died on Valentine's Day in 2000. I built the horse on top of a base that had casters. I used our loading dock to move the clay figure to the foundry when I was done later in 2004. The bronze mare now stands on the road leading up to my house in Vermont. I named her *Gertie,* after my mom.

After completing my bronze horse, I realized I'd benefit from a teacher's instruction, and I was fortunate to soon find Susan Clinard, a wonderful sculptor who taught at the Art Institute of Chicago. Susan agreed to take me on as a private student at her huge studio on the Near South Side of Chicago. I wanted to sculpt realistic, posed figures in clay to be cast in bronze and then mounted on tree branches. I loved the idea of integrating the characters with elements of nature.

It was Susan who taught me how to actually "see" a figure. When we were both looking at a model, what she saw and what I saw were not the same thing. She taught me how to see the subtle forms, curves and shapes from a sculptor's perspective. I went on to study with Susan Clinard for four amazing years.

I also prepared everyone at BMT for my retirement. Eighteen months before I turned sixty-five, I stepped down as the head of the company and installed Don Rosenwinkel as the new president. I was there if help was needed with the transition, but all of our clients and talented employees embraced Don, and my beloved company moved forward seamlessly.

I had enjoyed a marvelous, joyful career for forty-one years with mostly happy memories. Designing playthings to entertain and inspire children is a unique job. I loved my profession and always gave it everything I had. I never felt that playing for a living from age twenty-four to sixty-five was work. I had been incredibly lucky to meet Ed Zagorski and have my life play out as it did. But I didn't retire from the toy business—I *left* the toy business behind me—and became a sculptor. The day I left the toy business I thought of myself only as a sculptor.

As my sculpting improved, I decided to offer my pieces for charity. I was involved early on in fundraising for the new Comer Children's Hospital at the University of Chicago. In addition to state-of-the-art care for children, Comer was dedicated to having the hospital filled with artwork for the children, doctors, staff, and parents. I decided to sculpt and have a showing of my work and give half of all my sales to Comer Children's Hospital.

I wanted to create some sculptures of children for the fundraiser. To that end, Comer put me in touch with the parents of a little boy whose life had been saved by the hospital. The boy's parents brought him over to Big Monster Toys in 2005, and he was outwardly a typical three-year-old running around the studio. He couldn't sit still, and I must have taken a hundred photos, but he finally sat down for one second, and that was the shot I used for the pose. He wore blue jean bib overalls and a little T-shirt.

My first sculpture show, "Forms from Nature," was held September 9, 2006, at the Winter Garden atrium on the rooftop of the beautiful Harold Washington Library Center in Chicago. My friends and family were there, as well as many people who supported Comer Children's Hospital. My fourteen-inch-tall bronze sculpture showed the little boy sitting down. I mounted his figure on a small maple tree section. It was the hit of the show.

I decided to cast ten additional reproductions of the little boy, and I sold them all before the show even opened. I made one more copy of the little boy and mounted him on a five-foot-tall maple tree section so he sat at eye level. This piece was auctioned off to benefit the hospital, and my sculpture of the little boy is permanently displayed at Comer Children's Hospital. After this, I did another bronze sculpture of a little boy sitting on a swing that hangs from a branch. This figure also was auctioned off and is on permanent display at the hospital. All of this was going while I was still running Big Monster Toys. After the show, I stepped down as president of BMT and made Don Rosenwinkel head of the toy design company.

In spite of my success with bronze sculpture, I knew it was time for a change.

I didn't know where my sculpting was headed, but I knew instinctively that I would no longer be doing bronze figures. It was not creative enough for me. Working in bronze is mostly about execution. Once I decided on a pose and built the framework, it was about making the clay look like the model or the photograph.

One morning I was out for an early morning run along Lake Michigan, watching the sun come up in the far distance where the water touched the sky. There were just enough clouds to make the opening show of that particular morning a bright burst that stopped me in my tracks. Watching the birth of a new day was glorious. When I turned around, there was a fallen tree next to some stones. I certainly would have run by it if I hadn't stopped to look at the sunrise. It was an epiphany for me. I decided I would begin to create abstract pieces of sculpture with small stones affixed to the ends of wood branches. It was that simple—it just happened. I was open and ready for a new direction, and there it was. It was just like deciding to flip some plastic ants into a little pair of pants.

I went back later with my beat-up Ford 150 pickup truck to collect fallen tree branches and some stones. I stopped at Home Depot to buy a chainsaw. For the next three years, I created perhaps thirty or forty tree, stone, and boulder sculptures. What I loved was that where I started was never where I ended up. My work was always a surprise. I found a notable branch or tree section, removed the bark, then sanded and finished the beautiful maple. I started looking for trees on my property that had died but not yet fallen to the ground where water and insects would start to turn them into soil.

I sold some pieces, and although I didn't have the financial success I'd enjoyed with my bronze sculptures, my new work brought me great joy. I sold some small pieces to individuals and a few larger, outdoor pieces—one to a spa in Southern California and one to the East Bank Club in Chicago. Indoors, wood can last forever, and I thought that if I applied enough layers of urethane, I could protect wood from the outside elements. But I learned that wasn't possible. After a few years outdoors, water seeps into small cracks in the maple and the wood starts to rot from the inside out. I ultimately had to replace the wood sculptures at the California spa and the East Bank Club with new pieces made of stone and steel.

I realized that I had to change the medium I worked in if I was to continue creating outdoor sculptures. I chose steel to replace wood while retaining the stone and boulders. In addition to its permanence and durability, I found that working in steel allowed me to form curves and spirals and shapes that were not possible with the tree sections.

In 2012, one of my large pieces was accepted into a group show in Chicago's Lincoln Park. The two-ton boulder and steel structure would be outdoors and on location for four months. I titled it *New Day*, and after four months on display in Lincoln Park, it found a permanent home at the Research Park at the University of Illinois. *New Day* was dedicated to professor Edward Zagorski on his ninety-second birthday, September 20, 2013. On this same weekend, I was awarded the University of Illinois' Comeback Award. I rode in a convertible in a parade and was honored at a ceremony during halftime of Saturday's football game.

As my sculpting career took off, I searched for a public relations company to represent my work in the media, and found Sheila King PR in Chicago. In 2013, she started pitching staff at the Willis Tower, formerly known as the Sears Tower. The second-tallest building in the United States at the time was renowned for publicly displaying original art in its lobbies and atriums. Sheila connected me with Angela Burnett, who was responsible for choosing the artists to display their work in the atrium on the Wacker Street side.

When Angela and I inspected the building, I mentioned that much of my work was too large for the atrium. She suggested placing some of the pieces outside, which would be a first for the tower. We worked out the date and budget. Willis Tower paid for the trucking, crane, and installation.

When the show opened on April 22, 2015, it was the Willis Tower's first indoor/outdoor sculpture show. The installation took place over two days and Sheila King arranged for the local news outlets to cover the heavy equipment moving my steel and boulders into place. You couldn't turn on a Chicago television news program that weekend without viewing the installation of *Bolder and Boulder*. That fall I opened my own sculpture gallery on Fulton Street on the West Side of the city.

When I'm in Chicago, I work seven days a week at my studio. I'm an early riser and usually get there at 6:00 a.m. I'm home by early afternoon. I love being a sculptor, just as I loved designing toys. After more than five decades of productive and imaginative work, I can confidently say that creativity is a function of pressure. Creative people do what they do because they have to—it's what drives them. They feel the pressure, whether internal or external, of having to give life to their ideas in a positive way.

Creativity isn't finite. The toy design business isn't competitive in the way that some businesses are—we weren't simply trying to sell our product more inexpensively than our competitors. In a creative business, it helps if you build an environment that's conducive to inspiration and imagination. That's why our offices always displayed flowers and toys and were decorated in bright, cheerful colors. It's best if you work cooperatively with each other, not competitively.

The essence of our success was that we created and designed toys and games and dolls and we did it well. We knew the toy business. Our customers constantly needed new products. Our inventors needed clients coming in for presentations so that they would face a deadline. Marvin's idea to bring the designer into the client presentation to show his or her own product was absolute genius. There was no greater feeling in the world for a toy designer, model maker, or engineer than to hear a client say during a presentation, "Why didn't *I* think of that?"

When I took over as the managing partner of Marvin Glass & Associates after that horrific day in 1976, I immediately became an inventor-turned-businessman. I never aspired to run a multimillion-dollar company. At heart, I remained a toy designer and never stopped creating new toy ideas.

I had the good fortune of taking over a successful company with a profitable business model, and I didn't screw it up. Marvin was a skilled and dynamic businessman, but he also taught me what not to do. I didn't change our business strategy, but I quickly changed our office culture for the better. We worked far fewer hours relative to our workload, and we became more successful with happier partners and employees.

I still love to work, just as I did when my grandpa Jacob and I built a shoeshine box so I could start my first business when I was five years old. I loved to work then, and I love to work now. Bringing my imagination to life has allowed me to build toys and games that delight children and their families many years after I invented them. It's led me to prosperity and given me the opportunity to explore and enjoy our magnificent world. Most importantly, I've enjoyed many friendships and been blessed with a wonderful family. I've always been healthy, but today I'm in the best shape of my life, thanks to my daily Pilates, aerobics, and boxing lessons. I plan on celebrating my wonderful good fortune by going to work today.

Afterword

by Edward J. Zagorski

In the late seventies, I was still teaching at the University of Illinois and had the bright idea of inviting some outstanding graduates to give a lecture to our current students to stimulate them with their stories and the various opportunities available after they graduate. Four graduates would be invited each year during the month of April, and the school would pick up the tab for travel, motel, and food. The series of lectures would be called "On Building a Better Mouse Trap."

In the fourth year of the talks, Jeffrey Breslow, an outstanding graduate, gave his talk, entitled "Toy Design: Why Grow up?" He was in good company that year. His lecture was followed by Bill Stumph, who was the designer of the Aeron Chair. His lecture was entitled "The Humble Object."

I list these two graduates because they had both been caught up in my own Mouse Trap, which was an exhibit of primary design solutions in the corridors of the Art and Design Building. I put up these displays to show off the best of the best work of my sophomore design students, attempting to trap some unsuspecting youngster into becoming an industrial designer. It caught Bill Stumph, and it certainly trapped Jeffrey Breslow.

To get your designs into my Mouse Trap case was more meaningful than grades; if you made the case, you had accomplished something. This strategy was no mere ploy to exhort students to work; on the contrary, it scared the hell out of most of them. It was, in essence, a standard of quality for all to measure them against.

In 1977 we had the pleasure of having Neil Armstrong as our keynote speaker for the national conference of the Industrial Designers Society of America. The bulk of his talk was on the Polish scholar Nicholas Copernicus. Armstrong did not stress the physical and technical aspects of the moon landing, but instead emphasized the centuries of thought and imagination that made the lunar adventure possible. The project sprang out of the speculations and philosophy of men who had never seen a rocket or an electrical system, but without whose input we would probably still be decorating caves today perhaps with Magic Markers or aerosol cans.

At the end of his talk, Armstrong asked for questions, and a hand shot up from a young student studying industrial design: "What field would you advise today to study in anticipating future needs?"

Neil Armstrong's surprise answer had nothing to do with aviation, space, technology, design, or computers. Neil said, "Character—human character. This is the area where we've made the least progress—learning more about the brain, about our behavior, and the ways we relate to one another. I think that's the most important direction we can take—mainly to begin to understand ourselves."

Lewis Mumford, at the age of eighty-eight, wrote, "The test of maturity for nations as well as individuals is not the increase in power, but the growth of self-understanding, self-control, and self-direction. For a mature society, the man himself and not his machine or his organization is the chief work of art."

I think that Jeffrey Breslow is the epitome of Neil Armstrong and Lewis Mumford's expectations. Jeffrey thinks clearly, leading to thinking independently. Thinking independently leads to living confidently, and living confidently leads to living courageously. Living courageously leads to living hopefully.

Every college has an obligation to its students, an obligation to develop their abilities to think and live. (A part of this is a quote from an essay on liberal arts by William Deresiewicz). One of the greatest compliments that I received from a young student was when he walked up to me and said, "Zagorski, you don't teach design, you teach us how to live!" That was Jeffrey Breslow.

Imagine someone gathering the birthdays of all their friends and cohorts, eventually numbering over six hundred, and sending every person a birthday gift that they created, packaged, and mailed out, and doing this for twenty-five years. And coming up with a new gift idea every year, so that they ultimately created twenty-five different gifts. That's what Jeffrey did. My wife Vee and I were in the Brez Birthday Club for twenty-five years. He never missed a birthday.

Jeffrey has traveled all over the world to experience its natural wonders and has hiked thousands of miles on trails in the wilderness. Many of these hikes were for charitable causes and raised lots of money. When not hiking, he was doing other types of adventure travel.

In 1996, my wife and I joined Jeffrey and a group he put together called the Brez Adventure Club. For ten years before our trip, the Brez Adventure Club was just guys rafting, riding horses, hiking, and SCUBA diving. For the next decade it was co-ed. The trip my wife and I went on was whitewater rafting through the Grand Canyon, a seven-day trip that still thrills me when I think about it.

Jeffrey and I have been in a book club together for all these years. We are the only two members. We share books that we fall in love with. Recently we were having lunch in Champaign, which we often do, and an old Annie Dillard book came up that Jeffrey recommended that I read back in 1999: *For the Time Being*.

I sent a small book to Jeffrey in 2000 with the unusual title *One Good Turn, A Natural History of the Screwdriver and the Screw*. Not exactly a bestseller, but both of us have always been interested in tools. One of my industrial design projects was to pick a hand tool and design and then build a new handle.

A year later, for my eightieth birthday, Jeffrey made a surprise gift for me. It was a three-foot-by-three-foot wall hanging consisting of eighty old wooden-handle screwdrivers that he mounted in a beautiful spiral starting from the largest down to the smallest. I found out he spent weeks at flea markets in Chicago finding eighty of these particular tools.

By now you got the idea that birthdays were a big thing for The Brez. There's more!

In 2006, for my eighty-fifth birthday, Jeffrey put together fifteen of my former students from Illinois to contribute and pay for a bronze bust sculpted of me. He had me sit for Susan Clinard, a well-known Chicago sculptor. Jeffrey studied figurative sculpture for four years with Clinard but didn't feel confident that he could capture me. But Susan did.

Jeffrey arranged for my bronze life-size bust to be permanently placed in the Fine and Applied Arts building just down the hall from my old Mouse Trap display case. He said the fifteen students wanted to honor me while I was still around. Getting a public institution to place a bust honoring a living person is no easy deal—dead, much simpler. This only happened because Jeffrey was persistent.

What happens after the bust is placed if that living person misbehaves and does something appalling? Does the institution remove the bust? You bet they do!

I surprised everyone. I'm still here ten years later, still (mostly) behaving and ticking very nicely, thank you.

In January 2011, Jeffrey announced to me that he was planning to host my ninetieth birthday celebration nine months hence on September 20, which is my birthday. He wanted to hold it in Champaign where we had met fifty years earlier. I had been working on my own memoir of my life as an industrial design teacher. I had already spent ten years writing and had six hundred pages with no end in sight.

I decided that I wanted to have the book finished and published for the party, to give away to former students and friends, so that gave me nine months to complete it. I found an excellent editor, and three months before the party, she told me not to write another word if I wanted the book finished in time.

My book, *Get Ten Eagles*, was finished and published for the party, and I signed seventy-five copies for all the guests at my ninetieth. Not only did Jeffrey throw an incredible party, but he got me to finish my book.

Two years later, Jeffrey was honored by his alma matter as a "Come Back Alum" during the homecoming weekend at the University of Illinois. He was one of three honorees chosen, and they made a big fuss over him that weekend on September 20, 2013. He was in the parade and on the football field at halftime and at lots of other events celebrating his accomplishments since his graduation in 1965. All of this happened at the same time we were watching the Illinois football team getting their butt kicked on my ninety-second birthday.

That incredibly busy weekend, Jeffrey donated one of his giant three-ton steel and stone sculptures to the University of Illinois and installed it at the Research Park in Champaign. The sculpture, titled *New Day*, has a permanent home at the Research Park. The bronze plaque on its base reads:

> *Dedicated to Professor Emeritus Edward J. Zagorski, my lifelong teacher, mentor, and friend on the occasion of his 92 nd birthday, September 20, 2013, with love, respect, and admiration.*
>
> *Jeffrey Breslow*

Jeffrey has always considered me his mentor. I was somewhat shocked because I never considered myself a mentor.

Teachers get paid for teaching. They mentor on their own time. I began to consider who my mentors were and found several: Henry Dreyfuss, Jay Doblin, George Nelson, Heinz von Foerster, Pine Tiapa, and last but not least, Jeffrey Breslow.

My memory of Jeffrey coming into my office back in 1961 is not too vivid, but the trap was set, and I got him! I really didn't know until many years later the effect I had on him that day, and I will leave it up to him to tell you his entrapment story.

—Edward J. Zagorski
December 2015

*Edward J. Zagorski died on January 10, 2021. He was ninety-nine and a quarter. Ed told me that little children, when asked their age, would tell you proudly they are three and a half or five and three-quarters. Ed told me when you reach ninety, you can start using fractions again. I met Ed in 1961 and he was in my life for sixty years as teacher, mentor, and dear friend. We shared our lives together and were never out of touch, with letters, emails, and constant personal visits.

About fifty of his friends, former students, and family gathered on his one hundredth birthday on September 20, 2021, at the University of Illinois in Champaign, to tell stories and share memories about Ed Zagorski. Because we were there, Ed was there with us.

—J.B.